# EVERYTHING YOU NEVER LEARNED ABOUT BIRDS

## Lore & Legends · Science & Nature
## Hands-On Projects

### Rebecca Rupp
### Illustrated by Jeffrey C. Domm

*A Storey Publishing Book*

Storey Communications, Inc.
Schoolhouse Road
Pownal, Vermont 05261

## Dedications

For my father, who loved birds, and for Randy,
who bought his boys binoculars.
*–Rebecca Rupp*

To my wife Kristen
*–Jeffrey C. Domm*

*The mission of Storey Communications is to serve our customers
by publishing practical information that encourages personal
independence in harmony with the environment.*

Edited by Gwen W. Steege and Amanda R. Haar

Cover design and illustration by Jeffrey C. Domm

Text design, text production, electronic retouching of photographs and illustrations, and selected illustration by Greg Imhoff

Indexed by Word•a•bil•ity

Printed in the United States by RR Donnelley & Sons Company
10  9  8  7  6  5  4  3  2

Library of Congress Cataloging-in-Publication Data

Rupp, Rebecca.
   Everything you never learned about birds / Rebecca Rupp;
illustrated by Jeffrey C. Domm.
        p.    cm.
   "A Storey Publishing book."
   Includes bibliographical references and index.
   ISBN 0-88266-345-3
   1. Birds—Juvenile literature.   [1. Birds.]   I. Domm, Jeff, 1958–  ill.
II. Title.
QL676.2.R87  1995
598—dc20                                                        94-21014
                                                                     CIP
                                                                      AC

# CONTENTS

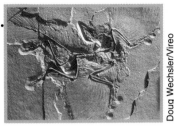
Doug Wechsler/Vireo

# FOREWORD

- What have you never learned about birds?
- What should you do with the baby Robin that drops from a tree onto your door step while your cat watches intently? (See page 15.)
- How did a pigeon win the US Army's Distinguished Service Cross? (See page 54.)
- Why do geese fly in a "V" formation? (See page 55.)
- How many people could you feed with a scrambled Ostrich egg? (See page 11.)
- What's the fastest bird? (Keep reading!)

Every day at the Cornell Lab of Ornithology I'm asked questions like these from folks across the country. If I'm at a loss to answer a question, out comes my birder's handbook, then its a call to the Lab ornithologist, and occasionally I find an answer by talking with a child.

Now wait a minute, you say. Talking with a child?

Yes, if you've never tried it watch out. Kids are just waiting for a chance to share all the cool things they've learned. And they know more than baseball stats and the names of mutant turtles. Here's an example:

I made a bird trivia game on my computer for an open house at the Cornell Laboratory of Ornithology, and one of the questions was "What's the fastest bird?" The possible answers included: Peregrine Falcon, Eagle, Robin, and Hummingbird. The question was met with a number of uncertain guesses and one very assured "none of the above" from a 12 year-old boy. I confess, at the time I thought: "that's not a choice, don't ruin my game." This young man then shared with me that although the Peregrine Falcon is regularly credited with being the fastest bird, seen diving past a plane at over 200 mph, there is actually a faster flyer. A species of swift, more specifically, the White-throated Needle-tailed Swift of Asia, has been credited with attaining a ground speed of 219 mph. That was a new bit of wisdom to me and certainly not something I ever expected to learn from a child. (See page 47 for more information on flight speed and by the way, if anyone knows of a faster bird feel free to write me.)

So how does a 12 year-old boy learn something that a "trained professional" doesn't?

Innate childhood curiosity motivates them, parental encouragement guides them, and on occasion, informative and fun children's books speak to them. *Everything You Never Learned about Birds* is one of these rare books.

I learned more than a few things (and enjoyed a chuckle with many more) from Rebecca Rupp's book. In addition, I came away with over a dozen great activities to share with my son — fun activities that will teach him meaningful things about birds and nature. I encourage you to spend an evening with this well-written and informative book and discover the answers to a few of your own questions about birds. Shared with an adult or a child, it's a fascinating and factual read. Enjoy!

Tim Dillon
Education Associate
Cornell Lab of Ornithology
159 Sapsucker Woods Road
Ithaca, NY 14850

# A BIRD IS BORN

◄ Which came first...?

The first egg-laying reptiles, very distant ancestors of the average backyard sparrow and bluebird, showed up on earth about 280 million years ago. Back in those days — the time of tree-sized ferns and foot-long dragonflies — the eggshell was a terrific new invention. Tiny embryonic reptiles were encased in a tough leathery protective eggshell, a shell that kept water in and everything else out. These new shelled eggs are called *cleidoic eggs,* from the ancient Greek word *kleido,* which means *locked up.* And locked up is exactly what they are. Cleidoic eggs are stubborn little survival packages. Without them, animals would never have managed to live on land.

The first real birds only came along about 150 million years ago — which means that the egg had at least a 130-million-year head start on the ancestor of the chicken. The egg came first.

## The Oldest Birds

Modern birds, many paleontologists now agree, are descended from the dinosaurs. The oldest known fossil specimen of a bird showed up in a limestone quarry in Germany in 1861, discovered by workers cutting stones for use in printers' shops. Scientists named the bird Archaeopteryx, which means ancient wing. Archaeopteryx lived about 150 million years ago. It was about the size of a raven and, like a bird, was covered with feathers and

had wings. It also, like a reptile, had pointy teeth, claw-tipped "fingers" (on its wing tips), and a long bony tail.

Shell-less eggs, such as those of amphibians and fish, must be laid in water, are smaller and simpler than eggs laid on land, and there are many more of them. Female frogs, for example, may lay as many as 30,000 eggs in a single breeding season. A female octopus may lay 150,000 eggs; a female flounder, a million eggs; and a female cod, nine million. These huge numbers of eggs are laid to ensure that at least a few offspring will manage to live to grow up. Usually the parents don't stick around to take care of their eggs, so most get eaten by predators before the babies hatch.

## INTRODUCING THE EGG

When most of us think *egg,* we think *chicken's egg* — the kind that (fried) looks up at you like a big googly eye from your breakfast plate. These are the eggs that you shouldn't put all in one basket or count before they hatch. Chickens generally lay about an egg a day, which — considering all the effort that goes into making an egg — is no mean trick. The egg starts out small, as an *ovum* in the *ovary* of a hen. In the ovary, the ovum begins to accumulate yolk proteins, which are made in the hen's liver, until it becomes big and ripe enough for release. Usually only one yolk is released by the ovary each day. If two ripen and are released at the same time, the hen lays a double-yolked egg.

### Millions of Eggs

The world champion egg-layer is the American oyster, which lays about 500 million eggs each year.

The yolk moves into the funnel-like end of the *oviduct,* a long twisting tube that acts as an assembly line for eggs. The first part of the oviduct is called the *infundibulum* (say *that* three times, fast), which is where fertilization takes place if the hen has mated with a rooster. Only fertilized eggs can develop into baby chicks. (The eggs you eat for breakfast are generally unfertilized eggs.)

Next, the yolk moves into the *magnum.* The inside of the magnum is a series of spiralling folds (think of the stripes on a barber pole) that cause the yolk to rotate as it moves along. Here, the rotating yolk is coated with layers of egg white. The very first layers of egg white are particularly dense and sticky, and as the yolk turns, they twist into long strands called *chalazae.* These strands help suspend the yolk and its developing embryo, so that it won't bash against the inner wall of the shell if the egg is jostled. The chalazae are the egg's version of a seat

## When You Wish upon an Egg

An old superstition says that a person who finds an egg with two yolks should make a wish while eating it.

## Map of an Egg

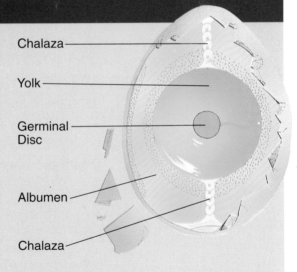

Chalaza

Yolk

Germinal Disc

Albumen

Chalaza

**1. Yolk.** The yolk (if people with forks don't get there first) is intended as food for the growing chick. The yolk is about half protein; the rest is fats, sugars, vitamins, and antibodies from the chick's mother. Antibodies are special chemical substances that protect the newly hatched chick from disease until its own immune system starts working. Much of the fat in the yolk is *cholesterol.* There's some scientific evidence that cholesterol may contribute to heart problems in humans, so most doctors warn people against eating too many egg yolks.

**2. Germinal disc.** You may be able to see a tiny little whitish spot near the middle of the yolk. This is the germinal disc — the living part of the egg. In fertilized eggs, it develops into a chick.

**3. Chalazae.** These twisted strands of protein are the seat belts of the egg. They

protect the yolk and the developing chick embryo from jostling.

**4. Albumen.** The egg white or albumen makes up about two-thirds of the egg's weight. It consists of protein and water. The egg white also contains a special active chemical called *lysozyme.* Lysozyme is an enzyme that kills off any bacteria that sneak in through the eggshell.

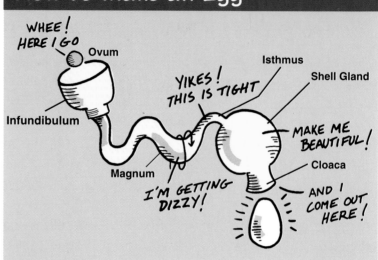

## How to Make an Egg

WHEE! HERE I GO

Ovum

Infundibulum

YIKES! THIS IS TIGHT

Isthmus

Shell Gland

MAKE ME BEAUTIFUL!

Cloaca

Magnum

I'M GETTING DIZZY!

AND I COME OUT HERE!

belt. You can see the chalazae in an uncooked egg, if you break an egg carefully into a shallow bowl. They look like twisty white coils on either side of the yolk.

Next, the egg is squeezed into the narrow *isthmus*, where the inner and outer shell membranes are laid down. At first these membranes fit the egg very tightly (like a pair of Spandex bicycle pants), but soon they stretch and loosen. The egg then moves into the *uterus*, or *shell gland*, and prepares to get its shell.

# HOW IS A BIRD'S EGG LIKE A CLAM?

Eggshells, like clam shells, oyster shells, and limestone, are made mostly out of calcium carbonate crystals. The average chicken eggshell weighs about 5 grams and about half of that is calcium. That's a *lot* of calcium. Birds can't possibly get enough calcium in their diets to produce a nice, solid eggshell, and scientists wondered for years about where all that calcium came from. Finally, they figured it out. The mother birds get it from their own bones.

Bones aren't solid all the way through; many have tunnels and cavities in the center that are filled with a soft, meaty substance called *marrow*. (That's why cave people used to crack open the bones of mammoths — to get

# A Very Strange Way to Shell an Egg

Place a hard-boiled egg in a jar or cup and cover it with vinegar. Soon you'll see little bubbles forming on the surface of the egg. These bubbles are made of carbon dioxide — the same gas that puts the fizz in soda pop. They form because a chemical reaction is taking place between the acid in the vinegar and the calcium carbonate in the eggshell. Leave the egg in the vinegar overnight. The shell will gradually dissolve, leaving behind a soft, rubbery hard-boiled egg.

at the juicy marrow.) That's where red blood cells come from: They're made in the marrow of your bones. Egg-laying mother birds, scientists found, have a lot of special extra bone. Many tiny spikes of this special bone — called *medullary bone* — grow into their marrow cavities, like the stalactites and stalagmites in caves. These little bone spikes are stockpiles of extra calcium. As the eggshell packs on calcium, growing bigger and thicker, the little spikes of medullary bone grow smaller and begin to disappear. A hen can use up as much as ten percent of her own bones in making eggshells.

The eggshell isn't a solid sheet of calcium carbonate crystals. If it were, the growing chick inside wouldn't be able to breathe. Eggshells are really full of holes. You can see these tiny pores with a magnifying glass. Try it. The

## It's a Fact!

The ancient Greeks recommended ash of eggshells mixed with wine as toothpaste.

**Bird Bone**

**Human Bone**

Human bone — like yours — is heavy solid stuff, filled with **marrow**. Bird bone, in contrast, is very light — often hollow. Bird bones are strengthed by extra little cross pieces of bone called **struts**. Mother birds may also grow extra internal spikes and knobs of bone called **medullary bone**, whiich is used as a source of extra calcium while making eggshells.

A Bird Is Born **5**

## An Egg of Your Own

You can use the vinegar reaction to make a mystery egg. With a white wax crayon, write your name, your initials, or a secret message ("HELP! I'M TRAPPED!") on the surface of your hard-boiled eggshell. Place the egg in vinegar. Leave it there for only four hours. The wax will protect the calcium carbonate in the shell from the vinegar reaction. The shell of the average chicken egg is about one-tenth of an inch thick. After four hours, about half of this will have dissolved away, leaving your message in raised letters on the surface of the shell.

### Ornithologist

An ornithologist is a scientist who studies birds. The word comes from the Greek word for bird, *ornis*.

pores look like tiny dimples on the surface of the shell. A chicken egg has about 10,000 of these pores — or 200 pores per square centimeter. (That's an area about the size of your little fingernail.)

## TINAMOUS LAY RED, ROBINS LAY BLUE

The last step in the making of an egg is the addition of color. Although most of the chicken eggs sold in supermarkets are white, some are brown, and there are breeds of chickens that lay green, blue, or yellow eggs. The American robin lays eggs of such a distinctive shade that a whole color has been named after them: robin's-egg blue. The flightless Australian emu lays dull green eggs that turn a shiny black a few days later. The South American tinamous lay beautiful glossy eggs in shades of green, blue, red, purple, and brown. The Northern flicker

C.B. Moore/Cornell Lab of Ornithology

◄ Find the eggs

lays eggs covered with mysterious-looking brown scribble marks, from which it gets its nickname, the "writing master." Owls, woodpeckers, and hummingbirds lay white eggs; blackbirds and sea gulls speckled or spotted eggs.

The blue and green colors in eggs come from cyannins, which are bile pigments. (Bile, which is made in the gall bladder, is used by your body to digest fat.) The reds, blacks, and browns come from chemicals called porphyrins, leftovers from the breakdown of old, used-up red blood cells.

Scientists aren't absolutely sure why birds' eggs are colored. Some egg colors are easy to explain: Spots, streaks, and speckles are for camouflage. A brownish speckled egg, for example, doesn't show up very well against a brownish speckled background of sand, twigs, or grass, and so it stands a better chance of escaping the hungry eyes of egg-munching predators. White eggs are generally laid by birds whose nesting places are particularly well hidden. Owls, who usually nest in hollow trees, lay white eggs. One reason for this, some scientists suggest, may be that white eggs show up well in the dark — which keeps the mother owl from stomping on them by mistake. Other egg colors are a puzzle. Nobody is really sure why robins' eggs are blue.

Blue?

# HOW MANY EGGS?

The reason farmers can trick their chickens into laying an egg a day is that chickens are *indeterminate layers.* That means that chickens will just keep on producing eggs, trying to accumulate a certain number — a *clutch* — in their nests. Most chickens are aiming for a clutch of twelve to fifteen eggs. As their eggs are taken away to go into scrambled eggs, French toast, and chocolate chip cookies, they continue to lay, trying to reach this magic number. Other birds are *determinate layers:* They lay only a certain number of eggs no matter what. If an egg is stolen or smashed, it's gone for good; the mother bird doesn't replace it.

# SHAPED LIKE AN EGG?

"Egg-shaped" to most of us means shaped like a chicken's egg — which really isn't at all fair. Eggs come in many different shapes and sizes. Egg-shaped to an owl means round; egg-shaped to a hummingbird means elliptical; and egg-shaped to a murre (rhymes with *purr*) means a sort of stretched pear with a pointed end. Murres have a good reason for laying such odd eggs. Murres are sea birds who breed in large colonies, containing hundreds or thousands of birds, on rocky ledges

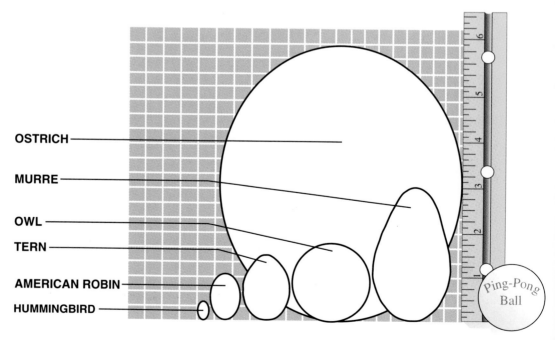

OSTRICH
MURRE
OWL
TERN
AMERICAN ROBIN
HUMMINGBIRD
Ping-Pong Ball

of ocean cliffs up toward the North Pole. Murre eggs are laid right on the bare rock of the ledge, but their shape prevents them from rolling off the edge. A rolled murre egg simply circles around on its pointed end. In fact, it's next to impossible to roll a murre egg in a straight line. If murres laid round eggs, it would be a whole different story. Think of a thousand ping-pong balls balanced on the edge of a table.

# Strong as an Egg

People think of eggshells as fragile. There's even a kind of fine china called *eggshell* china because it is so thin and delicate. Actually, though eggs can't survive falling off a cliff, they are a lot tougher than they look. Eggs are strong because they are shaped like domes. In a dome, weight pressing down from on top doesn't all squash down on any single point. Instead, the weight is shared: It travels down around the curved sides to the widest part of the dome, so that it is spread out over a larger area. Architects, who design buildings, simply love domes. A dome is a great way to have a lot of open space inside a building without needing lots of pillars or supporting

## ▼ The Architectural Egg

Capital Building, Washington D.C.

St. Maria Della Salute, Venice

## How Strong Is an Egg?

Crack two raw eggs in such a way that you get four approximately equal eggshell halves. Set these halves on a table, wide side down, in the shape of a square, one half at each corner. Put a book on top of them. What happens? Try another book. How high can you go?

The ability of the dome shape to distribute weight gives an eggshell more strength than you'd expect.

walls in the middle to hold it up. Planetariums are dome-shaped. The United States Capitol building in Washington, D.C., is dome-shaped.

The egg *has* to be strong, because it has to spend the next several days, weeks, or months supporting the weight of an adult bird sitting on it. An ostrich egg, for example, has to be strong enough to support the weight of a parent ostrich — usually the father ostrich, who can weigh up to 350 pounds. Chicken eggs, on the other hand, only have to worry about a 4-pound hen; while the tiny hummingbird egg (about the size of a big blueberry) is sat upon by an equally tiny parent, weighing only a fraction of an ounce. The egg of the hum-

## Eggs in Space

There you are, on top of a cliff, and you've got to get your egg safely to the ground below. Go for it. Build a device that will allow you to drop an egg safely off a cliff. Test your invention out with a *real egg*. Drop it out of a second-story window.

A Russian rocket scientist came up with one solution to this problem. The scientist's name was Konstantin Tsiolkovsky, and he was born in 1857. Tsiolkovsky had read a science fiction novel by Jules Verne called *From the Earth to the Moon*, in which moon-bound space travellers were protected from the shocks of take-off and landing by a waterbed-like cushion of water beneath their spaceship floor. Curious as to whether or not this would really work, Tsiolkovsky tested the cushioning effect of water on eggs. The prob-

lem, he found, was to keep the egg from either floating to the top or sinking to the bottom of his water-filled container. Here's how he solved it:

Stock Montage

1. Put an egg in a glass jar or plastic container half full of water.

2. Add salt until the egg floats.

3. Very carefully add fresh water, so that it forms a layer on top of the salt water. (If you add a little food coloring to the fresh water, you'll be able to see the separate layers.) The egg, which floats in salt water and sinks in fresh water, should sit safely between the two water layers.

4. Cap your jar and bang it on the table. Your cushioned egg shouldn't move.

100 CHICKEN EGGS!

ELEPHANT BIRD EGG

OSTRICH EGG

25 CHICKEN EGGS!

◀ World's Biggest Eggs

mingbird is the world's smallest bird's egg; the egg of the ostrich the world's largest. The average ostrich egg is 6 to 7 inches tall and 4 to 6 inches wide — about the size of a short football — and weighs 2 to 3 pounds. It is equivalent in weight to about twenty-five chicken eggs, which means that one scrambled ostrich egg would serve breakfast to about twelve people. (If you want your ostrich egg hard-boiled, you'd have to boil it for two hours.)

Big as the ostrich egg is, the world has seen even larger. The all-time champion giant egg was laid by the now-extinct elephant bird of Madagascar, a 10-foot-tall flightless bird whose monstrous egg was the size of a beach ball. It weighed about 27 pounds.

The important thing about egg size, though, is not how big the egg is itself, but how big the egg is in relationship to its mother, the egg-layer. A mother ostrich weighs about fifty times more than her egg. A mother hummingbird weighs about eight times more than her egg. This means, relatively speaking, that hummingbirds have bigger babies than ostriches. In these terms, biggest of all is the egg of the New Zealand kiwi, a flightless chicken-sized bird with shaggy fur-like feathers. The kiwi weighs only four times more than her egg, which, in people terms, would be like a 60-pound kid laying an egg as big as a watermelon.

## Walk on Eggs!

"To walk on eggs" is an expression meaning to walk very, very carefully over delicate ground. In Lima, Peru, though, you can *really* walk on eggs. In Lima, a bridge known as "The Bridge of Eggs" was built in 1610, using mortar mixed with the whites of 10,000 eggs.

WHEW!

The ancient Egyptians built immense incubators of clay bricks. These brick incubators, heated by fires, were capable of hatching 10,000 eggs at a time. The eggs were used to feed the workers who built the pyramids.

# HOW LONG TO HATCH?

How long does it take to hatch an egg? That depends on the type of bird. Chicken eggs hatch in about twenty-one days. The blackbird is the fastest hatcher — eleven days from egg to bird — and the royal albatross is the slowest, at seventy-nine days. It takes heat to hatch an egg, and in the Bird Family, this heat usually comes from a warm parent bird, sitting. Most of us think of the mother bird as the prime egg-sitter, but in many species the father pitches in and helps, too. As a rule of thumb, ornithologists say, in species in which the male and female are the same color, both parents take turns incubating the eggs.

Wild birds lay their eggs in the spring, and if you're cautious and careful, you may be able to observe a nest of eggs and keep watch until the baby birds hatch. One warning though: Never, EVER handle wild birds' eggs or remove them from their nests. You don't want to upset the parents or damage the young birds. (Besides, it's illegal. So, hands off!)

# BRINGING UP BABY

If you've ever seen a chick hatch, you know that a chick comes out of its egg pretty much ready to fend for itself. Chicks, like ostriches, ducks, and sea gulls, are *precocial* birds. Precocial birds are developmentally advanced: They hatch with their eyes open, are covered with special soft feathers called *down*, and are already able to run around and find food for themselves. Most small songbirds, on the other hand — robins, bluebirds, and sparrows, as well as owls, woodpeckers, pigeons, penguins, and parrots — are *altricial* birds. The word *altricial* comes from the Latin *altrix,* which means *nurse.* Altricial birds need a lot of care and nursing from their parents in order to survive. (Just like you did. If you were a bird, you'd have been altricial.) When altricial birds hatch, they are blind, naked, and helpless, and they look like newborn mistakes. About all they can do is lie in the nest and scream at the top of their lungs for food.

It's no small job to feed a brand-new bird. The great tit feeds its babies 900 times a day. Some small birds feed

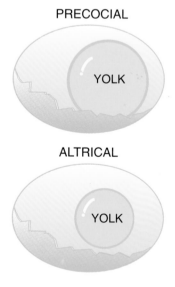

PRECOCIAL

YOLK

ALTRICAL

YOLK

Precocial birds, born open-eyed and ready to run, come from eggs with bigger yolks than do altrical birds, who are born blind and helpless.

their screeching infants forty times an hour — that's once every minute and a half. Most birds don't have it quite that bad: The usual feeding schedule is more like twenty times an hour — a leisurely once every three minutes. Parents feed their babies by instinct: The wide-open mouths of the baby birds, often brightly colored or patterned on the inside, send out the signal "Drop food in this NOW!"

Most parents take care of the babies until they're able to fly and leave the nest. Some young finches and warblers are out and on the wing in just eight days, but most growing birds take a little longer. Young swifts spend three to six weeks in the nest; and young albatrosses (the ones who take so long to hatch, remember?) need parental care for six long months. Some birds, like the skylark, the short-eared owl, and the corn bunting, boot their young out of the house even before they learn to fly: The unhappy bounced birds hang around in the shrubbery, begging for food. The parents ignore them, and eventually they accept adulthood and fly off on their own.

So why are some birds born tough and independent, and some weak and helpless? It all has to do, scientists say, with the availability of food and the number of baby-bird-eating predators. Precocial birds tend to be born on the ground, in poorly protected, easy-to-get-at locations — which is why they're born ready to run for their lives. Precocial birds come from eggs with bigger, richer yolks. A

## Home Alone

The megapodes — a group of large turkey-like birds, including the brush turkeys of Australia — don't sit on their eggs at all. Megapode mothers lay their eggs in huge mounds of sand and rotting vegetation, which may be 30 feet across and 5 to 7 feet high. Several females lay their eggs in the same mound. The eggs are kept warm by the sun and by heat generated by the decaying plant material. The father birds keep an eye on this warming process: Males continually monitor the temperature of the mound by taking samples with their beaks. If the mound seems too cool, they pile on more layers of sand and leaves; if too warm, they scratch holes in the top. All care ends, though, once the buried eggs hatch. Newborn chicks claw their way to the surface and go about the business of growing up, without further help from their parents. This, ornithologists believe, is the most primitive form of nest-building and egg care, very similar to the nest-making habits of the birds' ancient reptilian ancestors.

precocial bird's egg is about half yolk. The yolk is food for the growing embryo, and it takes more of it to make a well-developed precocial bird. The eggs of altricial birds, which get short-changed on food, are only about a quarter yolk. If chickens were altricial birds, your breakfast fried egg would have a dinky little yolk about the size of a penny.

# THE HISTORICAL EGG

Historically, eggs have meant more to people than just some yellow stuff to eat for breakfast. Eggs, for centuries, have been symbols of birth and new life. An ancient Hindu legend tells how the earth hatched out of a golden egg. The ancient Egyptians believed the sun hatched from an

## Egg Talk

If you're a nice person, people may call you a good egg; if you're not quite so nice, you might get labelled a bad egg, or — worse — a rotten egg; and if you're a serious student, people may call you an egghead, which should be a compliment, but doesn't sound like one. If somebody eggs you on, they prod you to hurry up and do something. If you get egg on your face, you've made a fool of yourself somehow. If somebody tells you to go lay an egg, they think you've just told a whopping lie; and in the theatre, if a play lays an egg, it's a flop. If you have absolutely no hair, you may be considered bald as an egg; if you're tough and heartless, you may be called hard-boiled; and if you're named Egbert, you probably keep it a secret.

# How to Hatch Your Own Eggs!

Since you're not as well equipped as a hen for sitting on a nest to hatch your own eggs, you'll need an incubator. Small inexpensive electric incubators are available from many scientific companies (see Appendix).

Incubated fertilized eggs must be kept at an even temperature of 100°F. Make sure your incubator is set correctly before adding fertilized eggs. The eggs must be turned over at least every 12 hours, to keep the growing embryo from sticking to the inside of the shell. Mother hens do this with their beaks and keep track of turning times in their head. You might want to keep a check list and mark one side of your eggshells with an X, to make sure the eggs get turned on schedule. You can often get fertilized eggs from farms. If you don't know a farmer, try the Yellow Pages of the telephone directory under "Eggs." Twenty-one days later: CHICKS!

Brower Manufacturing, Model THI10, Houghton, IA

---

## Lost and Found

If you find a lost-looking baby bird on the ground, don't rush immediately to the rescue. Back off, leave the bird alone, and keep an eye on the area for an hour or two to make sure no parent birds are around. Chances are that there are, and if so, they're a lot better at taking care of baby birds than you are.

If the young bird has obviously fallen from its nest, pick it up and gently replace it.

If your bird, however, turns out to be a genuine orphan, you've got your work cut out for you. First, you need to keep your bird warm. Make a nest in a small box, lined with soft shredded paper or bits of cloth. You'll probably need to place the nest under a light bulb to make sure your bird stays warm enough. Featherless babies need to be kept at about 95°F; down-covered birds at about 80°F. Bird infants need to be fed about every 15 minutes during the daytime. Use an eyedropper for feeding.

### Food for Infant Orphan Birds

2 tablespoons water

2 tablespoons milk

2 beaten egg yolks

baby cereal

liquid vitamins

Mix water, milk, and egg yolks together. Cook at medium heat in a double boiler for about ten minutes. Add enough baby cereal to thicken the mixture (about 2 tablespoons). Add 2 drops of liquid vitamins.

For more information, call your local veterinarian or wildlife officer.

# Make Your Own Pysanky

Pysanky kits, which contain egg dyes, patterns, kystkas (a special drawing tool), and beeswax, can often be found in art-supply stores. For sources, see Appendix.

You can also make your own homestyle pysanky eggs. You will need:

- White hard-boiled eggs
- Beeswax (available in sewing departments)
- Small metal container (bottle cap or jar lid)
- Pan or metal pie plate
- Pencils with erasers
- Straight pins
- Egg dyes or food coloring and cups

Put a small chunk of beeswax in the bottle cap or jar lid. Place this in a pan or pie plate and heat on top of the stove on low heat until melted. (Ask an adult to help with this, and be very careful. Wax is flammable.)

Stick a straight pin into the eraser end of a pencil. (This is your homemade kystka.) Dunk the head of the pin into the melted wax. Use the wax to drip or draw patterns on the surface of the eggshell. This will take time. You'll have to dip your pin again and again to draw a complicated design.

When you have finished drawing, place your egg in a cup of prepared dye. The wax design will stay white. When the egg is the color you want, take it out of the dye and let it dry. You can then wipe off the wax with a warm damp cloth or paper towel. Or add more wax, and dip the egg in a different colored dye. Repeat as many times as you like.

## How to Make a Diamond

An old British superstition claims that the yolk of an egg laid on Good Friday will turn into a diamond if kept for one hundred years.

egg; the ancient Polynesians said that the island of Hawaii hatched from an egg. The ancient Chinese gave eggs dyed red — the color of happiness — to children on their birthdays, or sent them to their friends as birth announcements. Many of us today associate eggs with Easter — which name comes from *Eoestre,* the Anglo-Saxon goddess of spring, who was often shown holding an egg in one hand. The custom of exchanging beautifully painted and gilded eggs as presents goes back thousands of years. In France, the king used to give decorated eggs to his courtiers on Easter Sunday, and by the 1700s, the common people were decorating and exchanging eggs too. In Poland and Ukraine, people make especially beautiful patterned Easter eggs called *pysanky.* Hot wax is dribbled onto the eggshell through a special tool called a *kystka.* Then, the egg is dipped in colored dye. More wax is applied, and the egg is dipped in a second color of dye. Layers of wax and dye are added until the eggs are covered with complex, beautiful designs. Some special symbols are used over and over: A sun means good luck; a chicken means wishes come true; a deer, good health; and flowers, love.

The most beautiful and expensive eggs of all time were probably those of Carl Fabergé, the nineteenth-century jeweler, who made the Imperial Easter eggs for the Czar of Russia. Made of gold, platinum, and colored enamels, and studded with jewels, the Fabergé eggs were richly and elaborately decorated. One egg, made in 1898, was over one foot tall, and contained a model of the Upensky Cathedral, where the Czar had been crowned. Another, made in 1902, contained a tiny replica of Gatchina Palace, in four colors of gold, trimmed with diamonds and pearls.

The most incredible eggs of all, though, are still the eggs laid every spring that miraculously develop, one by one, into a brand-new robin, bluebird, mockingbird, flamingo, ugly duckling, or swan.

The FORBES Magazine Collection, New York

A Fabergé Egg

# BOOKS FOR GOOD EGGS

## Fiction

Andersen, Hans Christian. ***The Ugly Duckling***. (Knopf; 1986)

*The classic story of the homely duckling who grew up to be a beautiful swan.*

Butterworth, Oliver. ***The Enormous Egg***. (Little, Brown; 1956)

*An unexpected egg from the family chicken coop hatches out an infant Triceratops.*

Edmondson, Madeleine. ***The Witch's Egg*** (Seabury; 1974)

*Agatha the witch finds an abandoned egg and hatches out a little cuckoo called Witchbird.*

King, Robin. ***The Wondrous Egg of Abou***. (E.P. Dutton; 1957)

*Abou finds an immense egg in the great desert and hatches out a troublesome baby ostrich with a "face of a great and beautiful foolishness."*

Milhous, Katherine. ***The Egg Tree*** (Scribner; 1950)

*The story of a Pennsylvania Dutch Easter, with instructions for making an egg tree of your own.*

Sans Souci, Robert D. ***The Talking Eggs: A Folktale from the American South***. (Dial; 1989)

*Blanche kindly gives a drink to a strange (and magical) old woman, who rewards her with the talking eggs.*

Sargent, Sarah. ***Weird Henry Berg***. (Crown; 1980)

*An ancient egg belonging to Henry's great-grandfather hatches a baby dragon.*

## Nonfiction

Cobb, Vicki. ***Why Can't You Unscramble an Egg?***
(Lodestar; 1990)

*Answers to a number of puzzling science questions, including an explanation of egg proteins and the changes they undergo when cooked or whipped.*

De Vito, Alfred. ***Exceptional Examination of Exemplar Experiments for Exciting Teaching With Eggs***. (Creative Ventures; 1982)

*Egg experiments for older kids, including how to make incubators from sandwich bags, calculate egg mass, and concoct egg shampoo.*

Griffin, Margaret, and Deborah Seed. ***The Amazing Egg Book***. (Addison-Wesley; 1989)

*Sixty pages of clever egg information and multidisciplinary activities.*

Hart, Rhonda Massingham. ***Easter Eggs by the Dozens!*** (Storey Publishing; 1993)
*Over 100 egg-decorating projects for artists of all ages.*

Lauber, Patricia. ***What's Hatching Out of That Egg?***
(Crown; 1979)

*Great photographs of various creatures hatching out of eggs, starting with a young ostrich.*

Penrose, Gordon. ***Magic Mud and Other Great Experiments***. (Simon & Schuster; 1987)

*Simple science experiments for younger kids. Several have to do with eggs, including "Green Sheep," in which kids sprout alfalfa seeds in emptied eggshells.*

# INNER BIRD, OUTER BIRD

Long ago in Greece, an ancient story goes, there lived a brilliant inventor named Daedalus. Daedalus had built a wonderful palace for King Minos of Crete, beneath which was a huge maze of mysterious tunnels — the Labyrinth — where the monstrous Minotaur lived. The Minotaur, half bull, half man, ate people and everybody was terrified of him. Finally, Daedalus and King Minos's daughter, the princess Ariadne, showed the hero Theseus how to find his way into the Labyrinth, where he killed the hideous Minotaur. Theseus and Ariadne then escaped by ship, but Daedalus was left behind. King Minos was so furious over the killing of his monster that he threw Daedalus into prison. Daedalus hated prison, and promptly came up with an invention that would allow him to escape.

He secretly made two sets of wings — for himself and his son, Icarus — out of feathers stuck into beeswax. He showed his son how to use the wings and warned him not to fly too near the sun, because the sun's heat would melt the wax and cause the wings to fall apart. Then Daedalus and Icarus leaped out of the window and flew away toward the island of Sicily. All would have been fine if Icarus had paid attention to his father's instructions, but he didn't. Instead, he flew higher and higher and closer to the sun, until, suddenly, the wax melted, his wings disintegrated, and he fell into the sea. Daedalus, brokenhearted, flew on to Sicily alone.

Don't worry too much about Icarus though — because this story could never have really happened. People wearing feathered wings would never have gotten off the ground. People are just too heavy.

## LIGHT AS A BIRD

For your size, even if you're skinny, you're still pretty solid. Say you weigh about 70 pounds. If a duck were your size — big enough to look you right in the eye — the duck would weigh only about 35 pounds, half your weight. Much of this difference in weight is due to differences in bones. The bones of furry animals (that includes you) are dense and thick, and filled in the center with a meaty substance called *marrow,* where new red blood cells are made. Bird bones are thinner and many of them

Hollow bones!

are hollow — filled with almost nothing but air. Though lightweight, these bones are still strong. Bird bones aren't completely empty, like drinking straws: They are supported inside by tiny crosspieces or struts, sort of like the spokes on a bicycle wheel. The air pockets in the bird's bones connect to the lungs, which means that when a bird breathes, air travels all the way down to its toes. The main function of these air pockets, or sacs, is to make the bird lighter

## ▼ Light Birds

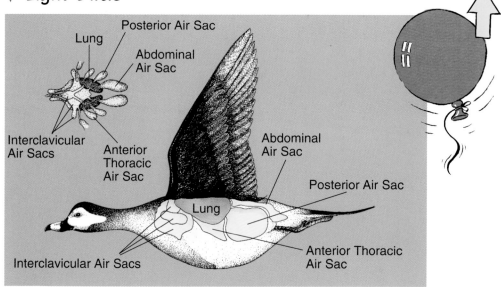

Posterior Air Sac
Lung
Abdominal Air Sac
Interclavicular Air Sacs
Anterior Thoracic Air Sac
Abdominal Air Sac
Posterior Air Sac
Lung
Anterior Thoracic Air Sac
Interclavicular Air Sacs

Air sacs may make up ⅕ of the body volume of a bird.

and more buoyant. If you think of people, for example, as solid rubber balls, birds would be balloons.

Hollow bones aren't the only way birds lighten themselves up for flight. Your heaviest collection of bones makes up your skull. People all have thick skulls, tough, protective cases for our invaluable brains. The heaviest part of the skull, however, is at the bottom: the jaw, filled with all those heavy, strong, white teeth. In birds, even the skull is pared down. The bones are thin and full of weight-reducing gaps or holes; and in place of teeth, birds have lightweight beaks.

## Heavy Birds

Not all birds have hollow air-filled bones. One exception is the loon. The common loon — the state bird of Minnesota — is a fish-eating water bird, with a daggerlike bill, black head, and black-and-white checker-patterned back. It's especially noted for its cry — a long, weird, yodeling laugh. The loon, which spends much of its time under-water, fishing, needs to be able to sink, so

its bones are solid. The heavy loon is a champion diver. Loons often dive to depths of 100 feet, and some have been nabbed in fishermen's nets 265 feet down in the Great Lakes.

Other water birds aren't quite so lucky. The hollow-boned pelican is so light that it has a hard time going underwater at all. Dunking a pelican is like trying to sink a cork.

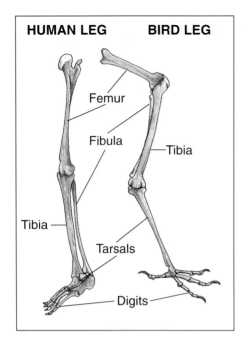

HUMAN LEG BIRD LEG

Femur

Fibula

Tibia

Tibia

Tarsals

Digits

# CONNECTIONS

Bird bones are not only lighter than yours; they're not put together in the same way. For one thing, birds don't have nearly as many joints as you do. Joints are places where two bones come together. They're the hinges of your body, places where you can bend, twist, and turn. Without joints, you'd be as stiff as a stick figure. The drawback of joints, from a bird's point of view, is their weight. Bones are broader and thicker at the joints, which means that joints can absorb a lot of force. (When you're running, for example, your knee joints can absorb a force up to seven times your body weight.) All this makes joints heavy, though, so birds have as few of them as possible. The vertebrae of your backbone are jointed, which makes you pretty flexible. Most of the vertebrae of a bird's backbone, on the other hand, are firmly fused together. Birds can't do backbends.

Birds can't kneel, either. The next time you see a (non-airborne) bird, take a good look at its legs. It looks like the bird's knees bend backwards. They don't really. What looks like the bird's foot is really just elongated toes. The long part of a bird's leg is a bone called the *tarsus*. On you, the equivalent bones, the *tarsals*, are the main bones in your foot, running from toes to heel. Birds actually walk up on tiptoe, and that backward knee is really a heel. True knees and thighs are tucked up out of sight, beneath the bird's feathers.

While all bird feet have some similarities, they're not all alike. The most common kind of bird foot is what sci-

## How to Walk on a Lily Pad

The jacana, a robin-sized wading bird of the tropical marshes, has extremely long toes, which allow the bird to walk across the water on top of lily pads. Jacanas are sometimes called "lily-trotters."

Tridactyl prints

Zygodactyl prints

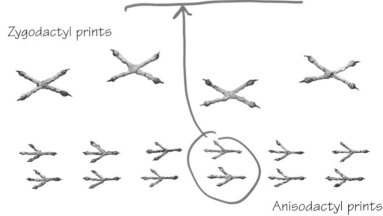

Anisodactyl prints

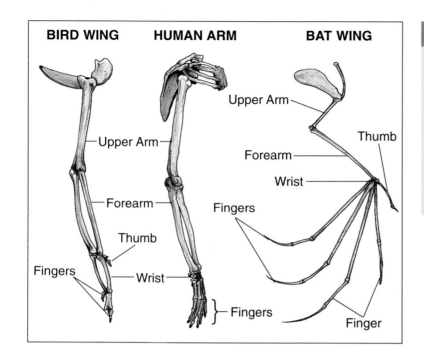

**BIRD WING**     **HUMAN ARM**     **BAT WING**

Upper Arm
Forearm
Thumb
Wrist
Fingers
Finger
Upper Arm
Forearm
Thumb
Fingers
Wrist
Fingers

## Did You Know?

In winter, the ptarmigan — the state bird of Alaska — grows special feathers on the tops and bottoms of its feet. These work like snowshoes, allowing the bird to walk across the surface of soft snow.

entists call an *anisodactyl* foot: three toes forward and one toe back — the sort of foot you would find on a chicken or a robin. Some birds, such as owls, cuckoos, parrots, woodpeckers, and roadrunners, have a more evenly divided *zygodactyl* foot: two toes forward and two toes back; their footprints look like the letter X. Plovers, auks, and guillemots have *tridactyl* feet — three toes only — and the heavy ostrich, who bounds across the African grasslands at 40 miles per hour, has only two toes.

Bird wings, in many ways, are a lot like human arms. The main bones of the bird wing are the *humerus* — the bone that on you reaches from shoulder to elbow — and the *radius* and *ulna,* the paired bones that on you reach from elbow to wrist. Birds don't have much in the way of fingers: just three small digits (one of them a thumb) at the ends of the major wing bones. (Bats, on the other hand, actually fly with their fingers. Bats have five long skinny finger bones, with skin stretched between them to form a wing.)

# KEELS AND WISHBONES

Flying requires a lot of muscle power. Birds get this power from their enormous chest muscles. Your chest muscles make up about one percent of your body weight; a bird's chest muscles, about fifteen percent of its body

## R͓: Owl's Feet

In medieval times, it was believed that the feet of the great horned owl, burned with herbs, would protect people from poisonous serpents.

## How is an Ostrich Like a Raft?

Not all birds have keels. One group of flight-less ground birds — including the African Ostrich, the Australian kiwi, and the South American rhea — have flat breastbones. Since these birds don't fly, they have no need for the huge chest muscles which, in airborne birds, attach to the protruding breastbone keel. Such keel-less birds are generally known as **ratites**. The name comes from the Latin **ratis**, which means raft — as in Huckleberry Finn's raft, a flat-bottomed vessel that also lacked a keel.

### When You Wish upon a Wishbone

The custom of breaking a wishbone to make a wish dates back to at least 300 B.C., to the oracles of the ancient Etruscans, who used dried wishbones of birds to predict the future. The wishbone custom was picked up by the Romans, who brought it to Great Britain. From there the early settlers brought the custom to America.

P.S. Scientists don't call it a wishbone. They call it a **furcula**.

weight. All of these powerful muscles need to be strongly anchored as they pull the bird's wings through the air. In birds, the flight muscles are anchored to the breastbone, or *sternum*. Flying birds have an enormously enlarged breastbone, with a keel — shaped like the keel on the bottom of a ship — sticking out in front. The powerful flight muscles are firmly fastened to this protruding keel. The flight muscles are also supported by the bird's wishbone. The wishbone is made up of a pair of *clavicles* (collar bones) fused together in the front for greater strength. Your collar bones aren't fused. (Feel them.) You don't have a keel or a wishbone. That's another reason why people can't fly.

## FEATHERS MAKE THE BIRD

The most important part of the outer bird — what really makes a bird, a *bird* — is feathers. Birds are the only animals with feathers. If you can grow feathers, you're a bird. The oldest feathers in the world, scientists believe, belonged to *Archaeopteryx,* a crow-sized bird (with teeth) who lived 150 million years ago — at the same time as *Apatosaurus* and *Tyrannosaurus Rex* (see page 2).

Feathers are much like reptilian scales or mammalian hair. All develop from special little pits, called *follicles*, in the skin, and all are made from a special chemical called *keratin.* Your hair, though, is simple stuff compared to feathers. A typical flight feather contains over one million precisely fitted parts. The hollow base of a feather, (the part that sticks into the bird's skin) is called the *quill.* The extension of the quill, (the stiff piece that runs up the middle of the feather), is called the *shaft,* or *rachis.* On

## Dissect a Chicken

Want to get a really good look at bird bones? The next time your family has roast chicken for dinner, save the chicken bones. After you've nibbled off all the chicken meat, scrape and clean the bones carefully and see how many you can identify. If you've eaten the chicken wings, for example, you'll be able to find the **radius** and the thinner **ulna,** which correspond to your lower arm bones, and the **humerus,** which corresponds to your upper arm bone. If you've had a drumstick, you've been gnawing on the *tibia*, or lower leg bone, which on you stretches from ankle to knee.

Go ahead and — in the name of science — poke through the leftovers. You should be able to identify **ribs** and **vertebrae,** the **sternum** with its large keel, the **furcula** (wishbone), the **femurs** (thigh bones), and the **pelvis** (bones of the hips).

either side of the shaft, (the soft part of the feather) are the *vanes*. The vanes are complex and clever pieces of engineering. Viewed up close, you can see that the vanes are made up of a series of feathery little branches called *barbs*. There are about 600 pairs of barbs on a single average feather. Off each barb are a series of even tinier branches called *barbules* — 500 pairs on each barb. And the barbules in turn are fringed with minute fibers called *barbicels*. The barbicels have little hooked tips called *hamuli* that interlock, zipping the barbicels, barbules, and barbs all together in a flat, flexible sheet.

### Comb Your Keratin!

Keratin is a long fibrous protein molecule made by skin cells. It makes up hair, scales, fur, and feathers, as well as spiderwebs, silkworm silk, fingernails, horns, beaks, and claws.

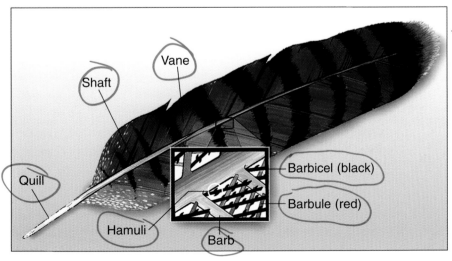

◄ **The Feather Up Close**

Vane

Shaft

Quill

Hamuli

Barb

Barbicel (black)

Barbule (red)

## Make a Quill Pen

In colonial times, the best feathers for making quill pens came from the wings of the barnyard goose. If you don't have a goose around the house, though, any large feather will do. You might try a feather from a turkey, crow, swan, or sea gull.

Pull off enough of the soft part of the feather from the broad end of the quill so that you can hold the quill comfortably for writing. Then, using a sharp knife — the colonists used special little *penknives* — cut the end of the quill in a curving slant, as shown.

Dip your pen in the ink bottle — not too deep, or you'll get blots — and prepare to write, just like John Hancock, Benjamin Franklin, and Thomas Jefferson.

1. Cut each edge

2. Cut the tip

"Oh, the hamuli are connected to the barbicels, and the barbicels are connected to the barbules..."

# FLIGHT FEATHERS, SEMIPLUMES, AND DOWN

Bird feathers don't just grow any which way. They usually grow in lines, or *tracts*, along the bird's body, with areas of bare skin in between. The feathers overlap, which is why birds appear to be completely feather covered. Your hair grows the same way: in lines, or tracts. That's why you can part it in a neat line.

Birds have six different kinds of feathers. The biggest, stiffest feathers, covering most of the adult bird's body, are called *contour* feathers. The most noticeable of these are the flight feathers — the big feathers of the wings and tail. Most feathers are attached to muscles, but the flight feathers, which need all the strength they can get, are fastened directly to the bones. Flight feathers aren't symmetrical. Usually one vane is much narrower than the other. The narrower vane curves down slightly: This is the outer side of the feather, the side that faces the wind when the bird is in flight. The wider, inner vane curls up slightly on the edge and faces away from the wind. In owls, who depend on sneak attacks to get their dinners, the outer edges of the flight feathers are soft and fluffy. The fluffy fringe keeps the feathers from snapping through the air, which allows the owl to fly silently.

Around the base of each contour feather grow *filoplumes* — hairlike feathers with just a few little barbs at the ends. They look like miniature feather dusters. Beneath the contour feathers is a layer of *semiplumes* and *down,* which function to keep the bird warm. Semiplumes look like unraveled contour feathers; they have a stiff central shaft, but soft fluffy vanes — they lack the little hooks that zip the barbules together. Down feathers look furry: They have tiny weak shafts and no vanes at all, just a cluster of long floppy barbs and barbules. Down is the bird equivalent of long underwear. Fluffed up, it traps air and insulates the bird in cold weather.

Less common feather types are *bristles,* hairlike feathers that grow around the bird's eyes, nostrils, and mouth, and *powder down,* feathers so soft and fragile that they crumble into powdery dust when touched. Bristles are thought to be organs of touch, sort of like a cat's whiskers. Powder down helps to waterproof and condition the other feathers and keeps the bird's skin dry. Pigeons, parrots, hawks, herons, and bitterns all have powder down.

## Feather Your Nest

Many birds line their nests with feathers to help warm the developing eggs. It is from this practice that we get the phrase "to feather one's nest" — which generally means to stock up goodies for yourself, often at the expense of somebody else.

"Mr. Badman had well feathered his nest with other men's goods and money."

—John Bunyan,
Pilgrim's Progress (1680)

## The Softest Bed

The world's most famous down is that of the eider duck. The mother eider lines her nest with soft, plushy down feathers plucked from her own breast. (Eider ducklings are the world's most pampered babies.) Eiderdown is so prized by people that eider ducks were once threatened with extinction by down-hunters. It makes a wonderful stuffing for pillows and comforters — soft, light, and warm. The word eiderdown, in fact, has come to mean a warm down-filled comforter. Down comforters and pillows nowadays are usually stuffed with goose down.

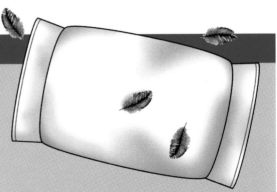

## ▼ Five Types of Feathers

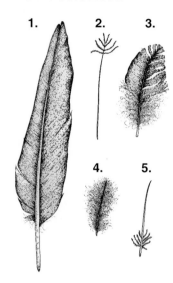

1. Contour feather
2. Filoplume
3. Semiplume
4. Down
5. Bristle

How many feathers does a bird have? The emperor penguin of chilly Antarctica, with 30,000 feathers, is probably the champion feather-bearer of the bird world. Runner-up, with 25,000 feathers, is the swan. The ruby-throated hummingbird, with fewer than 1,000 feathers, is at the bottom of the scale; the screech owl, with 6,500, somewhere in the middle.

# FANCY DRESS

Some of these many feathers are truly spectacular. Colored plumage is a quick and flashy way of telling other birds who and what you are. It's the bird equivalent of wearing a name tag at a political convention. A robin's red tummy, a woodpecker's red head, and a waxwing's yellow tail tip are all identification signals. The gaudiest feathers usually belong to the males and are used for sheer showing off. They're meant to tell available females, "Look at me! I'm great mate material!" Sometimes these fancy feathers appear only during the breeding season; sometimes the male gets to wear them all year long.

Some of the world's most famous feathers belong to the male peafowl, the peacock, who, for all his fancy plumage, is a relative of the plain old barnyard chicken. The peacock is practically all tail, which is 4 to 6 feet long. The spreading fan is made up of 200 huge feathers, each topped with a distinctive eyespot, colored blue, bronze, and green. Strictly speaking, the peacock's fan isn't a tail at all, but an array of enormous rump feathers — what

## Horsefeathers!

The ancient Greeks told stories of a mythical feathered horse: Pegasus, the winged steed who sprang (full-grown) from the blood of the snake-haired monster, Medusa. Horses other than Pegasus simply can't fly, which may be where we get the expression "Horsefeathers!" — which means "Rubbish!" and is used in response to any obviously silly statement. Teachers use it on kids who say the dog ate their homework.

ornithologists call "upper tail coverts." The peacock's real tail, short and drab, helps prop up the spread fan.

There's an old superstition that peacock feathers are unlucky, because of the eyespot, or "evil eye." Evil eye or not, the pharaohs of Egypt and the emperors of ancient Rome prized peacocks: Peacocks' brains were a favorite dish at Roman banquets. (So were camels' heels and parrot fish livers.) By the Middle Ages, people preferred their peacocks roasted whole. Castle cooks served them with all their tail feathers put back in place and a flaming brandy-soaked feather in their beaks. For hundreds of years, the peacock was the most expensive bird in Europe. In ancient Greece, where you could buy a rooster for 5 drachmas, a peacock cost 10,000. (The female peafowl or peahen, a dull brownish bird with no gaudy tail feathers, was luckier. People ignored her.)

Also famous for its plumes is the *quetzal*, once the sacred bird of the Aztecs of ancient Mexico. Today it is the national bird of Guatemala, where it even appears on Guatemalan coins — which are also called *quetzals*. The quetzal is only about one foot long, but has a wonderful 3½-foot tail of glistening emerald green feathers. Long ago, only kings were allowed to wear quetzal feathers. The birds-of-paradise of New Guinea and the Pacific islands also have beautiful plumes, of practically every size, shape, and color: lacy yellow plumes, velvety black feathers, feathers that form glittering bibs, fans, ruffs, or ballerina-like skirts. The Australian lyrebird has a huge, curved feather tail shaped exactly like a musical lyre. Herons and egrets are known for long flouncy white plumes called aigrettes or sprays that appear on their backs and breasts, usually in the breeding season.

## SOMETIMES IT'S BETTER TO BE BROWN

Most birds are more modest when it comes to feathers. Cleverly colored feathers, spotted, banded, and streaked in patterns of dark and light, make great camouflage. Many ground-dwelling birds have feathers in concealing shades of mottled browns and grays, designed to blend right into the brown-and-gray background. The speckled

### How the Redpoll Got His Red Head

A North American Eskimo legend tells that the redpoll, a little red-headed Arctic finch, was once a plain brown bird. Then, one very cold winter, he stole an ember from the ferocious bear who guarded all the fire in the world and brought it to the grateful Inuit people. His head has been red ever since from the burn of the stolen fire.

## How the Peacock Got His Tail

The story of the peacock's tail really began with Zeus, the king of the ancient Greek gods. Zeus had a wife, the goddess Hera, but he also had a terrible habit of wandering down to earth and marrying other women. This made Hera very angry, so Zeus did his best to be sneaky about his many love affairs. When he fell in love with the beautiful Io, daughter of the river-god, Hera nearly caught him, but Zeus, just in time, changed Io into a little white cow. Hera was suspicious about that cow, so she asked Zeus to give it to her for a present. Zeus didn't know how to say no, so Hera got the cow. She took the unlucky Io, tied her to a tree, and sent a servant to keep an eye on her. The servant was an excellent watchman. His name was Argus, and his body was covered with 100 eyes, at least half of which were wide-awake at all times. Zeus then sent Hermes, the messenger of the gods, to rescue Io. Hermes dressed up as a shepherd, sat next to Argus, and talked. He talked for hours. He told him a long, long, dull story, so dull that all 100 of Argus's eyes gradually closed. Forever. Hermes had bored Argus to death.

Hera was so upset over Argus's death that she took his hundred eyes and set them in the tail of the peacock, her favorite bird — and there they still remain today.

Io, who spent the rest of her life as a cow, ended up in Egypt, where the people worshipped her as a goddess.

Zeus kept on having love affairs.

bittern is a master/mistress of camouflage. This small wading bird stands stiffly upright among the reeds of its marshy home, its bill pointing straight up in the air. In this position, it is practically invisible — it looks exactly like a reed itself.

Some birds change their feathers to match the season. Arctic ptarmigans, for example, are a spotty mix of brown and black during the summer, but a pure snowy white in winter. Scientists call this *dichromatism* — which means *two colors*. These seasonal changes in feather color ensure that the feather-wearer will stay safely camouflaged all year-round. (Nonbirds exhibit dichromatism, too. The snowshoe hare, for example, turns white in winter and cocoa-brown in summer; Arctic foxes and weasels also change color with the seasons. The white winter weasel is called the ermine; lords and ladies of the Middle Ages wore robes trimmed with ermine fur.)

From a survival point of view, it's much better to be dull. Since prehistoric times, people have hunted birds

for their feathers — the brighter and more beautiful, the better. Hawaiian kings wore ceremonial helmets and cloaks of feathers, each of which might contain half a million feathers, plucked from 90,000 birds. African chieftains wore feather headdresses. Indians of the southeastern United States wore capes of turkey feathers; the Plains Indians were famous for their great eagle-feather war bonnets.

In the 1880s, an ornithologist from the American Museum of Natural History, on a stroll through the streets of New York City, spotted forty species of birds — all decorating women's hats. It was these fashionable hats that led to the founding of the Audubon Society. In the

## Feather Money

The natives of New Hebrides, a small group of western Pacific islands, used feathers for money. One honeyeater feather was worth one pig or two wives.

# ▼ Dichromatism

Dichromatism right

Dichromatism wrong

late 1800s and early 1900s, ladies wore hats whenever they left the house. Hats came in all shapes and sizes — for dressy occasions, they could be as big as cart wheels — and they were loaded with feathers. Especially popular were the feathers of herons, egrets, albatrosses, ostriches, and birds-of-paradise. Demand for feathers by the millinery industry was so great that plume hunters were paid $80 per ounce — which meant that feathers were worth more than gold. One auction house in London sold 48,240 ounces of heron feathers in a single year — which, right there, meant nearly 200,000 herons killed for their plumes. This wholesale slaughter of birds for hat feathers enraged many bird lovers and led George Bird Grinnell (his real name) to found the Audubon Society in 1886. Thanks to Mr. Grinnell, it is now illegal to wear wild bird feathers. The Audubon Society is still active today, working to protect birds and other wildlife.

Fashionable 19th-century lady's hat

## THE CHEMISTRY OF COLOR

The most colorful birds in the world are the parrots of the South and Central American rain forests. There are over 300 different species of parrots, and most are rainbow-bright, in shades of red, green, yellow, orange, purple, and blue. Some feather colors in birds come from special chemicals called *pigments. Melanins,* the same pigments that give you black skin or brown freckles, also give feathers their brown and black colors; *carotenoids* make red, orange, and yellow feathers. Birds can manufacture melanins inside their body cells; but they get their carotenoids at dinner, from their food. Red and yellow birds on a carotenoid-free diet turn white. When the Bronx Zoo flamingos start turning pale and bleached-looking, their keepers feed them red pepper and carrot oil — both full of carotenoids — to restore their bright pink feather color.

Other feather colors are due, not to chemical pigments, but to the special way in which the feather surface reflects light. There is no pigment for blue, as in bluebirds, blue jays, and indigo buntings. Instead, their feather barbules contain tiny particles that reflect light in such a way that the feather looks blue. Blue comes

The strangest feather color in the world may be that of the South American touraco. The touraco is a colorful relative of the cuckoo, which lives mostly on banana-like fruits called plantains. Touracos have bright red wings, due to a red pigment called **turacin**. Turacin contains a lot of pure copper — touracos are the only birds who get their color from copper — and, even stranger, turacin washes out in water. A dunked touraco loses its red color and ends up pale pink.

from the way the feather is built, not from colored chemicals. Green, as in parakeets, is a little bit of both, a combination of feather structure (blue) and carotenoids (yellow).

# THE NEW/GROOMED FEATHER

Feathers, on a bird, need a lot of tending. Birds take baths, in water or in dust, and they are constantly *preening:* rearranging ruffled feathers with their bills or beaks, re-zipping separated barbules, preparing the feathers for flight. Birds don't preen to make themselves look pretty; preening is an essential form of equipment maintenance. Don't think of a movie star primping in front of a mirror: Think of a flight mechanic readying a machine for take-off. Most birds have a special *preen gland* at the base of the tail, which, when pressed on, gives out an oily substance that birds smear carefully over their feathers. This oil keeps the feathers soft and flexible (think of hair conditioner) and, in water birds, keeps them waterproof.

## PROJECT

## Make a Birdbath

A discarded garbage can lid (provided there are no holes in it) makes a terrific bath for grubby birds. Set the lid in a shallow hole in the yard, so that the edges of the lid are level with the ground. Place a few stones in the birdbath — some birds like to wade in and out of the tub. Fill the bath about three inches deep with water. Remember to clean the birdbath often.

Chances are, the birds will find your bath as is, but you can make it even more irresistible by adding the sound of running, or dripping, water. Try hanging a plastic bucket, suspended from a tree on a length of

twine, above your birdbath. Fill the bucket with water and punch a tiny hole in the bottom, so that the water drips slowly into the bath below. Fill the bucket daily.

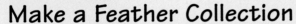

When water rolls off a duck's back, it's due to oil from the preen gland.

In spite of all this care, feathers eventually wear out. At least once a year, birds molt — that is lose their old, ragged feathers, and replace them with new. Molting usually occurs in the late summer or early fall, and may take several weeks. Flight feathers are generally lost two by two, in symmetrical pairs, so that molting birds are not left helpless and grounded. Some birds, though, like ducks, swans, and pelicans, are synchronous molters, which means that they lose their feathers almost all at once. During this period of rapid molting, the birds can't fly, so synchronous molters often make their feather changes in private hiding places, to keep out of the way of predators. At the end of the molt, the bird is as good as new, every barbicel, barbule, barb, and vane back in place, and ready to fly.

## Feather Phrases

If you're in full feather, you're dressed up fit to kill; if you've got a feather in your cap, you've done something to be proud of; and if you're a featherweight, you're tiny. If somebody calls you featherheaded or featherbrained, they mean you're empty-headed and silly. If they accuse you of featherbedding, they think you've been making things too easy on yourself and should work a little harder. If you get involved in a noisy fight, you may really make the feathers fly; and if somebody tells you, "You could have knocked me down with a feather!" it means they were completely flabbergasted.

# BOOKS FOR (NON)FEATHERBRAINS

Belting, Natalia.
**The Long-Tailed Bear and Other Indian Legends.**
(Bobbs; 1961)

*A collection of Native American tales, including "How the Birds Came to Have Their Many Colors," "Why Crane's Feathers are Brown and Otter Doesn't Feel the Cold," and "How Turkey Got His White Tail Feathers."*

D'Aulaire, Ingri, and Edgar Parin.
**D'Aulaire's Book of Greek Myths.**
(Doubleday; 1962)

*Includes the stories of Daedalus and Icarus, and of Pegasus, the (feathered) flying horse.*

Freeman, Don.
**Will's Quills.**
(Viking; 1975)

*The story of the goose who provided William Shakespeare with quills for pens.*

Geisel, Theodor Seuss (Dr. Seuss).
**Yertle the Turtle and Other Stories.**
(Random House; 1986)

*Includes the story of Gertrude McFuzz, a bird who gorges on pill-berries and grows an embarrassingly enormous feathered tail.*

Knudson, Barbara.
**How the Guinea Fowl got Her Spots: A Swahili Tale of Friendship.**
(Carolrhoda; 1990)

Leach, Maria.
**How the People Sang the Mountains Up: How and Why Stories.**
(Viking; 1967)

*How and why stories from many different cultures, including "Why the Birds Are Different Colors" and "Why Robin Has a Red Breast."*

Palacios, Agentina.
**The Hummingbird King: A Guatemalan Legend.**
(Troll Associates; 1993)

*The story of the quetzal.*

Peet, Bill.
**The Spooky Tail of Prewitt Peacock.**
(Houghton Mifflin; 1973)

*A spunky peacock uses his strange tail to frighten off a hungry tiger.*

Troughton, Joanna.
**How the Birds Changed Their Feathers: A South American Indian Folk Tale.**
(Peter J. Bedrick Books; 1986)

*The birds, once white, conquered a fearsome Rainbow Snake and take its colors for their own.*

# Soar Like an Eagle, Flap Like a Duck

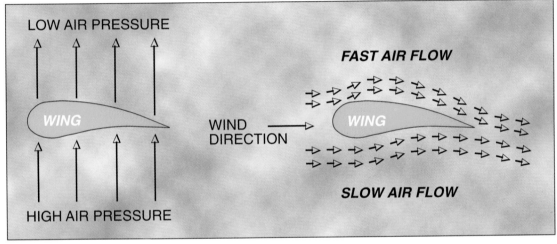

▲ Typical Airfoil

**I**f you *fly the coop,* you escape, run away, skip camp, or make a getaway. If you *travel as the crow flies,* you go in a straight line from one place to another. If you *fly in the face of disaster,* you meet trouble head on.

When a bird flies, though, it really takes to the air. Birds stay airborne basically for the same reason airplanes and kites do: All three are boosted upwards by air pressure. In birds and airplanes, this boost — officially known as lift — comes from the shape of the wing. Wings, looked at sideways, are roughly teardrop-shaped, with a longer, curved upper surface and a shorter, flatter bottom surface. When the bird (or airplane) launches itself forward, its wing cuts through the air like a fish cuts through water. The air separates, part of it flowing over and part of it under the wing. However, since the

In ancient Rome, the owl has flown was a slang expression for bribery. The phrase came from the Greeks, who used to stamp a picture of an owl on their coins. When those coins changed hands, the owl "flew."

top of the wing is longer than the bottom, the air has to travel faster to get across the top. (Think of two horses running around a racetrack. To keep from falling behind, the horse on the outside of the track has to run faster than the horse on the inside, because he has farther to go.) Fast-moving air generates less air pressure than slow-moving air, because in fast-moving air, all those heavy gas molecules are being rapidly whisked out of the way. So, as the bird moves forward, there's more pressure shoving *up* from the slow air underneath the wing than there is shoving *down* from the fast air above the wing. This difference in pressure makes the bird (or airplane or kite) go up. This is *lift*.

# GLIDE, FLAP, SOAR, AND HOVER

There's no one right way to fly, which is why birds come in so many different shapes and sizes. Birds may flap, soar, hover, or glide — or dive, tumble, roll over in midair, and do back flips. Baby birds apparently learn to do all this by themselves. There's not much evidence, ornithologists agree, for young birds being taught to fly. Birds fly by instinct, and instinct sometimes kicks into gear fast — as in a flat two seconds, after unexpectedly falling over the edge of the nest.

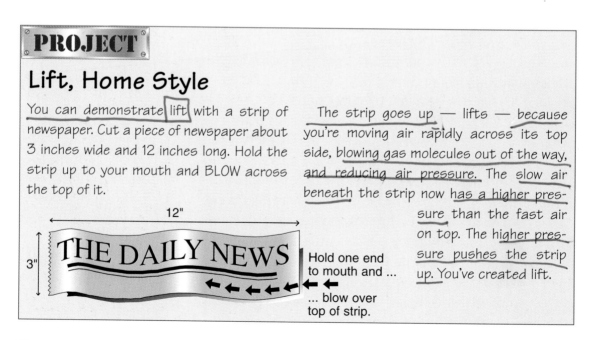

## PROJECT

## Lift, Home Style

You can demonstrate lift with a strip of newspaper. Cut a piece of newspaper about 3 inches wide and 12 inches long. Hold the strip up to your mouth and BLOW across the top of it.

The strip goes up — lifts — because you're moving air rapidly across its top side, blowing gas molecules out of the way, and reducing air pressure. The slow air beneath the strip now has a higher pressure than the fast air on top. The higher pressure pushes the strip up. You've created lift.

12"

THE DAILY NEWS

3"

Hold one end to mouth and ...

... blow over top of strip.

## All about Air Pressure

Air looks and feels like a lot of nothing, but don't be fooled. Air is a mixture of gases, mostly nitrogen and oxygen, plus some neon, argon, helium, hydrogen, and carbon dioxide. These gases are not only all around you; they're stacked up over you in a column six miles high. (Imagine a pillar of air as tall as Mount Everest sitting squarely on top of your head.) That much air is heavy. In fact, at sea level, it weighs 15 pounds per square inch.

Try this one. Lie down flat on the floor. Get somebody to measure how many inches long you are and (approximately) how many inches wide you are.

Now, calculate:

1. (number of inches long) X (number of inches wide) = square inches of you
2. (square inches of you) X 15 = number of pounds of air pressing down on you when you are lying flat

Woof. That's air pressure.

---

*Gliding* is the simplest kind of flight, largely a matter of spreading out flat in the air and entering into a slow, graceful fall. This, scientists guess, was the flying style of *Archaeopteryx,* who lacked the proper chest muscles for flapping. Flying fish, flying squirrels, flying lizards, and flying opossums all glide. Gliding, plus soaring, is the preferred technique of the vulture, the condor, and the albatross, birds too heavy to hold themselves up for long periods by flapping. Gliding is a lot like coasting on a bicycle, when your legs are too tired to pedal anymore.

*Flapping* is what most people think of when they think "bird flight." It's the usual flight style of water birds (ducks, for example, flap) and of small songbirds, like robins, bluebirds, and cardinals. Flapping isn't just a simple matter of waving wings up and down. The true flap requires precise positioning of the feathers. The biggies here are the *primary feathers,* the largest and stiffest of the flight feathers, that do the main work of shoving the flapping bird through the air. Primary feathers are attached to the digits of the wing, the bird equivalents of human fingers. As the wings sweep down, the feathers clamp together in an airtight seal, thrusting the bird forward. When the wings sweep back up, the feathers rotate open like the slats of Venetian blinds, allowing air to pass through.

The flapping wing twists under on the downstroke, forcing air to move faster over the *secondary* and *ter-*

### Bernoulli's Principle

Daniel Bernoulli, a Swiss scientist who lived from 1700 to 1783, was the first person to explain how faster air movement reduces air pressure and creates lift. This idea is known today as "Bernoulli's Principle."

Stock Montage

## ▼ The Flapping Process

*tiary feathers* — which make up the airfoil, or lifting, part of the wing. Secondary flight feathers are smaller than the primaries and are attached to the bird's *ulna* (on you, that's the bone that runs from your wrist to your elbow). Tertiaries are connected to the *humerus*, the elbow-to-shoulder bone.

## GETTING OFF THE GROUND

Not all birds are cut out to be flappers. The bigger a bird is, the more difficult flapping becomes. As a bird gets heavier, it needs more and more lift to boost it into the air; therefore, its wings get wider and larger — and heavier and harder to move. The wings of the tiny hummingbird, which weighs about as much as a penny, only account for about one-twentieth of its total body weight. The wings of a 5-pound heron, on the other hand, make up about one-fourth of its body weight; and an 8-pound eagle has one-third of its weight in wings. The largest flying birds nowadays are the bustards — relatives of vultures — of Europe and Australia. Bustards weigh a little over 30 pounds, which seems to be about the top limit for getting off the ground. Other heavy fliers include condors, albatrosses, vultures, and swans.

The bigger a bird is, the faster it has to fly to stay airborne, and the bigger and more powerful its chest muscles — which operate the wings — have to be. Really big birds, strong as they are, are hard put to flap fast enough.

Instead, they prefer to *soar*. Soaring birds get a lot of help from Mother Nature, riding wind currents and *thermals*, which are columns of warm air rising up from the earth's surface. Thermals generally don't form until mid-morning, after the earth warms up in the sun. This means that some soaring birds, like vultures, start the day late. Until the thermals start to rise, vultures stay on the ground. Sea gulls often depend on *obstruction currents*, which occur when the wind hits a large solid object, like a seaside cliff, and is pushed upwards. Gulls ride these rising splashes of air like surfers ride waves.

Big birds have particular problems with take-offs and landings. Andean condors, whose wings measure 10 feet across from wing tip to wing tip, can only take off from level ground in a high wind. Usually they launch themselves off the tops of cliffs. (South American natives sometimes catch condors by baiting windless valleys with food. The birds land to eat and then can't get back into the air.) The huge albatrosses of the Pacific islands were nicknamed "gooney birds" by sailors during World War II because of their foolish-looking take-offs and landings. Albatrosses have to run like mad to get airborne, and — without wind — they land in a skidding belly flop.

## A Kettle of Hawks

When a whole group of hawks rides a thermal together, they seem to swirl upward like the steam rising from the spout of a boiling tea kettle. That's why a bunch of hawks is called a "kettle."

## Air Surfers

Relying on strong winds and obstruction currents, sea gulls can soar effortlessly while scoping out the ocean's surface for food.

Hummingbird ► in Flight

Mike Hopiak/Cornell Lab of Ornithology

## Flapping Feats

| Bird | Wing Beats Per Second |
|---|---|
| Vulture | 1 |
| Red-tailed hawk | 2 |
| Pigeon | 5 to 8 |
| Mockingbird | 14 |
| Chickadee | 27 |
| Hummingbird | 80 |
| Honeybee | 250 |
| Gnat | 500 |

Very small birds have their problems, too. Smaller wings spread out over smaller amounts of air, which means less lift. To make up for this, smaller birds have to beat their wings faster. The immense, and usually soaring, vulture flaps its wings about once every second. Small land birds, like sparrows, flap about fourteen times per second, and tiny hummingbirds, who have to work hard to stay up, have the fastest wing beats of all birds: about eighty flaps per second.

The bee hummingbird of Cuba, the smallest of all birds, weighs about ⅕ of an ounce, less than a butterfly. Aerodynamically, the bee hummingbird and its bigger

## Dragons of the Air

The largest creature ever to have gotten itself airborne was Quetzalcoatlus, a short-tailed pterosaur (an ancient flying reptile) who lived during the Cretaceous Period, 140 to 65 million years ago. Quetzalcoatlus had a wingspan of 35 feet, which is about the same size as a modern-day executive jet.

Runner-up for largest flier was probably

Pterosaur

the related Pteranodon, with a 23-foot wingspan. Both had membranous wings, somewhat like giant bats.

hummingbird relatives really are more like bees than birds, with their buzzing wings and hovering flight. Hummingbirds fly with their bodies held upright, not lying on their tummies, like most birds. The hovering bird whips its wings forward and backward in a super-speedy figure eight. The wings of a hovering hummingbird work like helicopter rotors. Hummingbirds not only hover: They fly forward, backward, and upside down, and turn somersaults in the air. (But they can't walk.)

# FASTER THAN A SPEEDING BULLET

How fast does flapping make a bird go? Fast. The fastest land animal is the African cheetah who, for short stretches, can sprint along at 70 miles per hour. More usual cheetah racing speed, though, is around 43 miles per hour, about the same as a fast racehorse. When birds turn on the juice, they leave us ground-dwellers in the dust. Many birds, including the plump pigeon, can hit speeds up to 100 miles per hour, and some swifts, doves, falcons, and sandpipers approach 200 miles per hour. One excited bird-watcher reported seeing a peregrine falcon zip past an airplane doing 175 miles per hour, though the swifts, at up to 200 miles per hour in level flight, are generally thought to be the world's fastest flappers. A peregrine falcon's *stoop* is an exercise in sheer mind-boggling speed. A peregrine falcon prefers other birds — especially pigeons — for dinner; and it routinely nabs dinner on the wing, dropping down on it in a bulletlike whoosh from 1,000 feet up in the air. This rocketing dive is called a stoop — but *bomb* might be a better description. It ends with the falcon hitting the luckless pigeon feet-first, instantly breaking its back. Stooping falcons may reach speeds of 150 to 200 miles per hour, which makes them the fastest killers on record.

The peregrine falcon zeroes in on dinner, rocketing out of the sky at 150 – 200 mph.

## Bowse, Feak, and Warble

**Falconry** — the art of taming wild birds of prey and using them for hunting — dates back to ancient Egypt and China, though it was most popular in the European Middle Ages. There were strict medieval rules governing who could own which birds: eagles were reserved for kings; falcons, called noble hawks, were for members of the nobility; and goshawks, called ignoble hawks, went to the peasants.

Falconry had a language all its own. Female falcons were called *merlins*; males, *tiercels*. The birds were kept in a *mews* — a special birdhouse, or aviary — and were carried out to the hunting field on portable perches called *cadges*. The man who carried the cadge was called the *cadger*. (Because the cadger was usually an old falconer, some people think this is where we get our word *codger*, as in "He's an old

Stock Montage

codger.") There were special words to describe practically every falcon behavior. *To bowse* meant *to drink; to feak* meant *to wipe off the bill after eating. To rouse* meant *to shake the feathers into place; and to warble, to stretch out the wings.*

## Speeding Birds (etc.)

| Bird | Miles Per Hour |
|---|---|
| House sparrow | 10 to 20 |
| American robin | 20 to 30 |
| Herring gull | 20 to 40 |
| Crow | 31 to 45 |
| Ostrich | 45 |
| Hummingbird | 30 to 47 |
| Duck | 44 to 59 |
| Swift | 60 to 200 |
| Tortoise | 2 |
| Hare | 35 |
| Cheetah | 43 to 70 |
| Speeding bullet | 900 |

# THE HEART OF THE MATTER

Flying, at any speed, uses up a lot of energy, and to provide all this energy, birds continually run their internal engines on high. A bird's heart beats harder than that of almost any other animal: 400 beats per minute, resting, and 1000 beats or more per minute in flight. Your heart, when you're not doing much of anything, probably beats about 90 times a minute; grown-ups' hearts at about 70 times a minute. Birds' hearts are four or five times bigger than your heart, too, relative to their total body weight. Your heart is about the same size as your fist — but if you were a bird, you'd have a heart the size of a cantaloupe.

Birds also breathe faster than you do. When you're lolling around in the living room, you probably breathe about 16 times a minute; when you're really panting after a fast run, you may breathe up to 80 or 90 times a minute. A pigeon at rest, just puttering around the park bench, breathes 29 times a minute; an airborne flapping pigeon about 450 times a minute. For all this, birds never get out of breath. They get all the air they need just by flying into it.

Pass the active Muscle please!

Birds breathe so rapidly because their muscles work so hard — and hard-working muscles need a lot of oxygen. Oxygen gets to the muscles through the blood, carried, in both you and birds, by red blood cells. You have a *lot* of red blood cells — millions in every drop of blood — but birds have even more. Bird blood, in fact, has more red blood cells per ounce than any other blood in the world, which makes bird blood the world's best system for ferrying oxygen.

The more active a muscle is, the more oxygen it needs, and the more oxygen it needs, the more blood vessels it has to have. That's why (cooked) birds have light and dark meat. A turkey drumstick is dark because it's full of blood vessels. When you ask for dark meat at the Thanksgiving dinner table, you're zeroing in on active muscle. Chicken breast meat is white because it's a relatively inert muscle: Chickens don't use their flight muscles much, except for an occasional flutter around the barnyard. Ducks, on the other hand, who spend a lot of time athletically on the wing, have dark breast meat.

## RUNNING ON HIGH

All of this high-powered activity generates a lot of heat. Birds are hot. Your normal body temperature is 98.6°F; normal body temperature for a bird is usually 7 to 8 degrees hotter. Since birds ordinarily run so hot, they need special ways of cooling down. You cool down by means of your three million sweat glands: Sweat, evaporating off the surface of your skin, causes your body to cool off. (It may not feel like it after you've been racing around in the hot sun, but it's true.) Birds, however, have no sweat glands. Instead, they cool off from the inside out, through the internal system of air sacs that fills their chest and abdominal spaces and extends into their hollow bones. Up to three-quarters of the air a bird breathes is used just for cooling down.

### Pant! Gasp!

Overheated birds don't sweat, but some do pant. Herons and nighthawks for example, rapidly vibrate their throats to boost evaporation. This cool-down procedure—the bird version of panting—is known to ornithologists as gular fluttering.

Some hot birds simply head for the nearest puddle for a cooling splash and vultures, who have their own set of social standards, cool off by peeing all over their legs.

49

# WHY FLY?

Birds don't fly just for fun — they fly to survive. Flying is serious business, used for catching dinner and escaping predators. When birds no longer need to fly — that is, when food is right there on the ground and/or there are no enemies at hand — they quickly lose their flying ability. It makes no sense to crank out all that energy for no good reason. Still, of the 10,000 or so species of birds in the world, only forty-six can't fly. Prominent among non-fliers are the Antarctic penguins, who need to be heavy enough to dive for their dinner, and the enormous ground-pounding African ostriches. Flightless birds can sometimes be found living on remote, danger-free islands. One famous example is the now-extinct dodo, who lived on the islands of Mauritius and Réunion in the Indian Ocean. The dodo was so used to peace and quiet that it wasn't even afraid of people. The Portuguese and Dutch sailors who discovered its islands could walk right up to it and grab it by the neck. And did.

Stock Montage

▲ **The Dodo**

## SOUTH FOR THE WINTER

At the opposite end of the scale from the flightless dodo is the Arctic tern, which not only flies, but flies nearly 25,000 miles each year. The Arctic tern, a gull-like water

## Bird Play

Though flying is generally serious business for birds, essential for their survival, some birds do fly to play. Crows and ravens are particularly known for fooling around in the air. Much crow-and-raven play is based on a maneuver called a roll: Flying birds tuck in their wings and roll over on their backs for a second or so, just for the heck of it. Real daredevils do double rolls, or flips, in which the flipper reverses itself and abruptly ends up flying in the opposite direction.

## Birds Aren't the Only Ones

Birds aren't the only animals to migrate. Gray whales travel annually from Alaska to Mexico; bluefin tuna, from the Gulf of Mexico to Norway; green turtles, from Brazil to Ascension Island in the Atlantic Ocean. Eels, from both North America and Europe, make a yearly trek to their breeding grounds in the Sargasso Sea. Butterflies migrate: Painted ladies migrate from North Africa to Scotland and monarch butterflies from the northeastern United States travel south each year at the rate of 80 miles per day, to spend the winter in Mexico.

bird, is the world's champion migrator, travelling annually from the Arctic to the Antarctic and back again. (The Arctic tern may also be the world's champion sunbather: It spends eight months of every year in regions where the sun never sets.)

Not all birds migrate. In fact, most don't: Scientists estimate that only about fifteen percent of all bird species seasonally change their homes. The rest, including cardinals, woodpeckers, jays, house sparrows, nuthatches, and chickadees, stay put; and one unusual bird, Nuttall's poorwill, a western relative of the whippoorwill, hibernates. (The Hopi Indians call the poor-will "the sleeping one.") Most small North American songbirds — robins, bluebirds, finches, and thrushes — go south for the winter, usually travelling distances of 250 to 2,000 miles.

Scientists aren't quite sure *why* birds migrate. One guess is that the yearly move has to do with bird comfort: The migrators are looking for warmer weather and better food. Others claim that migrating birds are heading back to their ancestral homes. One theory holds that birds originated in the toasty tropics and gradually moved north, looking for more space and less competition from hungry neighbors. This became a yearly summer habit, but in winter, when the weather turns nasty, sensible birds still turn around and head south for home. Another theory holds that northern birds only started whizzing off

### Did You Know?

Though there are forty-six species of flightless birds, the world's only wingless bird is the kiwi of New Zealand.

## The Mysterious Disappearing Birds

The annual disappearance of the birds puzzled people for hundreds of years. Some thought that all the birds hibernated in winter, huddling together at the bottoms of ponds or rivers. One seventeenth-century writer even claimed that birds spent their winters on the moon.

southward in the days of the Ice Ages, to escape the creeping glaciers. Nowadays, when winter sets in, they remember their ancient escape routes and head toward warmer climates.

North American birds generally find their way south along one of four major "flyways"— bird versions of interstate highways. The most popular of these is the Mississippi River Flyway, which, since it runs right along the Mississippi River, is easy to spot from the air. Other flyways run along the Atlantic and Pacific coasts and down the Rocky Mountains.

North-south migration along these flyways is called *latitudinal migration,* because it runs up & down the ladder of the lines of latitude circling the globe. Not all birds, though, migrate north-to-south. Some migrate longitudinally: That is, they move east-west, changing lines of longitude. The hawfinch, for example, a classic longitudinal migrator, summers in Russia and in winter moves east to Japan. There are also up-and-down *altitudinal migrations,* like that of California's mountain quail. The quail nests about 10,000 feet up in the mountains during the spring and summer months; in the fall, in small groups walking single file, they descend to about 5,000 feet, where they spend the winter.

### Flyways of ▶ North America

The four major flyways are bird versions of interstate highways.

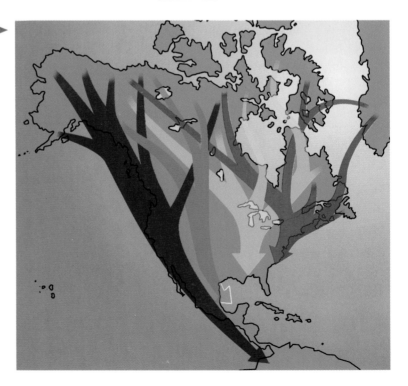

# Sun, Stars, and Magnetic Fields

*How* birds migrate is almost as much of a puzzle as why. Some birds seem to navigate on long journeys using landmarks on earth as guideposts. Others seem to pick up directional clues from the stars, the sun, or from the earth's magnetic field. Night-flying migrants, like the robin, the mallard duck, and the indigo bunting, are star-sighters: Experiments have shown that these birds recognize many of the constellations near the North Star, including the Big and Little Dippers, and the W-shaped Cassiopaeia. Day migrants, like petrels, albatrosses, and starlings, often calculate their direction from the angle of the sun's path across the sky. Some birds are able to orient themselves by sensing the earth's magnetic lines of force: Magnetic particles inside the birds' bodies are affected by the earth's magnetism. Robins and homing pigeons sometimes navigate like this, and so do dolphins, tuna, turtles, and honeybees.

Some feats of bird migration, however, are so incredible that they seem almost impossible to explain. A Manx shearwater — named for the British Isle of Man, home of the tailless Manx cat — was moved by airplane from its nest on an island off Wales to Boston, Massachusetts, a distance of 3,000 miles. Released, it was back home again in 12 days. Homing pigeons are famous for finding their way home: One champion ("Bullet") made it from Abilene, Texas, back to Fort Wayne, Indiana, a distance of over 1,000 miles, in a mere day and a half. Exactly how homing pigeons (or Manx shearwaters) manage to zero in on home remains a mystery. It was once thought that the pigeons simply had great memories: They remember and retrace their flight routes. However, experiments have shown that there's more to it than that. Drugged homing pigeons, transported great distances in their sleep, still make it back home. One pigeon-tester shut some pigeons up in a large closed drum, put the drum on a revolving turntable that spun around four times each minute, loaded the whole spinning setup on a truck, and

53

## The Bravest Bird

Homing pigeons were used to carry military messages during World Wars I and II, when they were sometimes called "winged telegraphs." The most famous of these was a pigeon belonging to New York's 77th "Statue of Liberty" Division — 550 soldiers fighting under Major Charles Whittlesey in France in World War I. In 1918, the 77th was up against the Argonne Forest, a powerful German stronghold, and their commander, General John ("Black Jack") Pershing, ordered them to advance "without regard for losses." The 77th bravely advanced — and ended up trapped on a hill, surrounded by enemy guns, unable to move. They had no food or medical supplies, and ammunition was running low. On their third day on the hill, to make matters even worse, they were bombarded by artillery from their own side. Major Whittlesey wrote a message pinpointing his position, added a note saying, "For heaven's sake, stop it!" and sent it off by his last pigeon, Cher Ami. (The name means *Dear Friend* in French.) Cher Ami, though wounded, got through, and the (friendly) shelling stopped. The 77th held out alone on their hill for five more days. The Germans demanded surrender; Major Whittlesey and his men stubbornly refused. When relief finally arrived, only 190 of the 77th's 550 soldiers were still alive.

## And the Rest of the Story

Major Whittlesey won the Medal of Honor.

Cher Ami, without whom he wouldn't have been around to receive it, won the Distinguished Service Cross.

Cher Ami lost an eye and a leg in this action — she eventually was fitted out with her own wooden leg.

transported the dizzy pigeons hundreds of miles. The pigeons weren't fooled. All returned home.

Not all birds are as talented as homing pigeons. Blue tits, transported as little as six miles away from their nests, get too confused to find their way home again. Even homing pigeons sometimes have their lapses: 100 Baltimore homing pigeons were once released in the Florida Keys and none of them ever returned home. Nobody knows what happened to them.

## Preflight Preparations

Birds prepare for migration just like bears prepare for sleeping through the winter: They eat. Some birds add 50 percent to their body weight before the trip. If a 70-pound kid were preparing to migrate, he or she would have to pack on an extra 35 pounds. Some birds even double their weight. The sedge warbler gets so fat that fat buildup under its eyelids keeps it from closing its eyes. Migration uses a lot of energy, and this new body fat makes for a very efficient fuel. One scientist calculated that if the lackpoll warbler burned gas instead of body fat, the bird would get 720,000 miles per gallon.

## The Valuable V

Migrating ducks and geese often fly in V-shaped formations, with the lead bird at the point of the V, and up to twenty-five followers flapping along behind. The V, scientists believe, is a way of saving energy during long migratory flights. Each bird flies in the upwash of its neighbor's beating wings, and this extra bit of supporting wind increases lift. Birds in a V can fly up to 70 percent farther than a bird on its own.

## Up and Away

During migration, birds fly high. The summertime bird, going about its daily business, usually sticks fairly close to the ground, venturing no higher than 500 or so feet, which is about the height of the Washington Monument. Migrating birds, however, generally fly somewhere between 5,000 and 20,000 feet, with the champion high flyers to date being a flock of whooper swans on their way from Iceland to their winter grounds in north Ireland. An airline pilot spotted them skimming along at 27,000 feet.

## SHOW YOUR I.D.

Bird banding (called *ringing* in Europe) is one of the major techniques ornithologists use to study bird movements and migrations. Bird banding has been going on for hundreds, even thousands, of years. In ancient Rome, spectators sometimes removed sparrows from their nests and took them in cages to the chariot races. There colored threads were tied around the birds' legs, the color indicating which driver had won the race. The sparrows were then released to return home, where eager chariot fans were waiting to see the race results.

27,000 FEET

20,000 FEET

5,000 FEET

500 FEET

In medieval times, falcon owners sometimes banded their hunting birds to show ownership. A story of a peregrine falcon belonging to King Henry IV of France tells of the bird escaping from the king's palace at Fontainebleau and being picked up the following day on the island of Malta, 1,350 miles away. The bird was identified by means of the gold ring it wore around its leg.

Bird banding was begun in this country by John James Audubon, the famous naturalist and artist. In 1803, Audubon discovered a nest of phoebes (small gray-brown-colored flycatchers) in a cave in the woods. He succeeded in taming the mother and babies, and eventually tried banding the little family with loops of thin silver wire. The banded birds returned to the same nest the following year.

Today over half a million North American birds are banded every year, each with an aluminum or plastic leg band stamped with a serial number. When and where the banded birds are recovered tells ornithologists a lot about bird behavior: where wintering and breeding grounds are located, what routes are used during migration, how long birds live.

## What To Do If You Find a Bird Band

Though nowadays no one is allowed to band a bird without a permit, under certain conditions you are allowed to take a band off. If you find a discarded bird band or a dead bird wearing a band, carefully remove the band, flatten it, and send it to:

Include your name and address, the date the band was found, the exact location where you found it, and the species of the banded bird.

If you find a live bird wearing a band, *don't* take the band off. Instead, write the serial number on a card, along with the information above, and send it to the Bird Banding Laboratory. Let the bird go.

BIRD BAND

U.S. Fish & Wildlife

Place Stamp Here.

NATIONAL BIRD BANDING LABORATORY
LAUREL, MARYLAND
20708-4039

Kids can participate in the Audubon Society's Christmas Bird Count. For forms and information, write to "American Birds" at the National Audubon Society (for address, see Appendix).

Nowadays not just anybody is allowed to band birds. Bird banding is regulated through the Bird Banding Laboratory (BBL), which is a branch of the U.S. Fish and Wildlife Service in Washington, D.C. To get a bird banding permit, you must be at least 18 years old. You must also be recommended by two qualified ornithologists and be able to show your ability to handle wild birds safely and to keep accurate records.

## COUNT THE BIRDS

Bird researchers also try to keep track of birds through annual population counts. Population counts are often conducted as cooperative research projects, in which volunteers all over the country collect information and send it in to a central organization. One of the best known of these cooperative projects is the Christmas Bird Count, sponsored each year by the National Audubon Society. Volunteers count the number of birds of each species seen on a single day within two weeks of Christmas. The information is used to learn about changes in the size of bird populations.

### Flight Phrases

If you're *flighty*, you're fanciful and irresponsible. If you're a *high flier*, chances are you're a party animal and a big spender, in which case, you may end up as a *fly-by-night*, or a person who sneaks out of town to avoid paying debts. If you're a *bird of passage*, you don't stay put for any length of time, but move constantly from place to place. If you *fly with the owls*, you like to stay up late at night.

# FICTIONAL FLIERS

Gerstein, Mordicai. ***Arnold of the Ducks.***
(Harper Collins; 1983)

*Arnold, kidnapped by a passing pelican, is raised with the family of Mrs. Leda Duck, dressed in feathers, and is taught how to fly and swim right along with the ducklings.*

Gormley, Beatrice. ***Mail-Order Wings.***
(E.P. Dutton; 1981)

*Andrea writes away for a pair of magic wings, and then falls into the hands of an evil scientist, who wants to turn her permanently into a bird.*

Holling, Clancy. ***Seabird.***
(Houghton Mifflin; 1948)

*A carved ivory gull — inspired by a real gull seen in an ocean storm — becomes the mascot for four generations in Ezra's family, on board a whaling ship, a clipper, a steamship, and finally, an airplane.*

Lagerlof, Selma. ***The Wonderful Adventures of Nils.***
(Doubleday; 1967)

*Nils is shrunk to elf-size by a passing elf and ends up flying away with the wild geese on their annual migration to Lapland.*

Langton, Jane. ***The Fledgling.***
(Harper; 1980)

*Eleanor and Eddy form a Protection Society to look after their little cousin Georgie, who has learned how to fly from a magical Canada goose.*

Snyder, Zilpha Keatley. ***Black and Blue Magic.***
(Atheneum; 1966)

*Harry Houdini Marco — always falling over his own feet — meets a sorcerer and is given a pair of magic wings.*

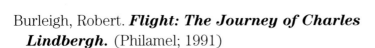

Burleigh, Robert. ***Flight: The Journey of Charles Lindbergh.*** (Philamel; 1991)

*A re-creation of the first solo flight across the Atlantic in 1927.*

Dagliesh, Alice. ***Ride on the Wind.*** (Scribner; 1956)

*The story of Charles Lindbergh and his historic solo flight across the Atlantic.*

Freedman, Russell. ***The Wright Brothers: How They Invented the Airplane.*** (Holiday; 1991)

*The story of the Wright brothers and their famous invention, lavishly illustrated with turn-of-the-century photographs.*

Provensen, Alice and Martin. ***The Glorious Flight.*** (Viking; 1983)

*The story of Louis Blériot and his famous flight across the English Channel.*

Quackenbush, Robert. ***Clear the Cow Pasture, I'm Coming in for a Landing!*** (Simon and Schuster; 1990)

*A short, clever biography of Amelia Earhart.*

Quackenbush, Robert. ***Take Me Out to the Airfield!*** (Parent's Magazine Press; 1976)

*The story of the Wright brothers' invention of the airplane, with simple instructions for building a model of The Flyer.*

# DINNER WITH THE BIRDS

YOU EAT LIKE A BIRD!

Nowadays when you tell someone that they eat like a bird, you mean that they pick at their food and barely eat anything at all. This is a misused phrase. To *really* eat like a bird, you'd have to spend all your days shamelessly stuffing your face. Birds have enormous appetites. The word *ravenous,* which means absolutely starving and ready to eat everything in sight, comes from the eating habits of the raven, a big and hungry relative of the crow. Magpies spend half their time eating. Hummingbirds eat about every ten minutes, slurping down twice their body weight in nectar every day. Most birds eat one-quarter to one-half of their body weight in food daily. To keep up with that, you'd have to munch your way through 175 peanut-butter-and-jelly sandwiches a day.

There are almost as many kinds of bird diets as there are birds. Robins eat earthworms; sparrows eat seeds; owls eat mice; herons eat frogs; and oystercatchers eat oysters. The Everglade kite eats snails; the albatross eats squid; the kookaburra of Australia (whose weird call earned it the nickname "laughing jackass") eats lizards. The elf owl of the American Southwest eats scorpions (first nipping off and throwing away the deadly stinger). The tawny eagle of Africa eats everything from locusts to dead elephants; and geese eat grass.

## PROJECT RLP Drip

# Feed the Birds

Feeding the birds isn't just a wintertime activity. You can enjoy watching birds at your feeder all year-round.

Here are some food picks for your feeder menu:

## Nuts and Seeds

Sunflower seeds, cracked corn, and millet are all bird favorites. If you buy commercial birdseed, make sure you're getting some of these in your seed mix. Birds also like melon, squash, and pumpkin seeds, so save the seeds from your breakfast cantaloupe and your Halloween jack-o'-lantern. Blue jays like corn right off the cob — put out some whole dried ears — and chickadees like coconut. Peanuts and popcorn are as popular at the birdfeeder as they are at the ball game; so are crumbled potato chips.

And, just like those feeder-robbing squirrels, birds like nuts. Collect acorns, hickory nuts, beechnuts, and walnuts. Before putting them in your feeder, smash them with a hammer, so that the birds can get at the meats.

## Fruit

Put out apple, pear, and orange halves (orioles and finches are especially fond of oranges). Many birds like grapes, which you should squash a little to make for easier eating, and fresh or frozen blueberries. Bluebirds, robins, catbirds, and mockingbirds all like raisins and currants, which should be soaked in water to plump them up before putting in the feeder.

## Breads and Cereals

Old-fashioned bread crumbs and crusts are just fine for the birdfeeder — and so are cookie crumbs, cracker crumbs, broken-up bits of muffin, and dry cereal. (Birds like Cheerios.) They also like oatmeal, raw or cooked.

## Extra Added Attractions

Some birds, such as warblers and orioles, like sweets; try putting out little saucers of jam or jelly.

Crushed-up eggshells are a good source of calcium. Save the shells from your breakfast eggs, smash them up, and put out in the spring for egg-laying mother birds.

## PROJECT

# Nectar for the Hummingbirds

Hummingbirds sip sugary nectar from flower blossoms, but they also like home-made sugar syrups. To make your own hummingbird food, mix 1 part white sugar with 4 parts water in a saucepan. Boil for 1 or 2 minutes. Cool the mixture and pour it into your hummingbird feeder.

If you don't have a hummingbird feeder, you can make your own. Fill a small jar to the top with your nectar and hang it from a tree branch or stake. Tie a red ribbon around the jar to get the hummingbird's attention. Hummingbirds love red.

H.P. Smith, Jr./Vireo

**WARNING:** Be sure you clean and refill your hummingbird feeder every two or three days, to prevent contamination with bacteria or fungi. If your nectar looks cloudy, get rid of it; it's contaminated. You don't want your hummingbirds to get sick.

## PROJECT

# George Washington's Breakfast . . . for the Birds

Every morning for breakfast George Washington used to eat three hoecakes, washed down with three cups of tea. Hoecakes are little flat cakes made from water, salt, and yellow cornmeal. In the early days of the American colonies they were cooked over an open fire on the flat blade of a hoe — that's why they were called hoecakes.

### Here's how to make some of your own:

1.  Bring 2 cups of water and ½ teaspoon of salt to a boil in a saucepan. Add ½ cup of yellow cornmeal, and simmer for about 1 hour, stirring occasionally. When done, you'll have cornmeal mush.

2.  Spoon the mush into a small loaf pan and refrigerate overnight.

    For breakfast in the morning, cut the mush into slices and fry it in butter.

3.  Serve with syrup or honey.

Once you've sampled George Washington's breakfast, share your hoecakes with the birds. Birds also like yellow cornmeal mixed with peanut butter.

# How to Serve Suet

Suet is beef fat, and insect-eating birds, like woodpeckers, flickers, nuthatches, orioles, and chickadees, love it. You can buy suet in chunks from meat markets, or you can prepare you own, using fat trimmings from steak or roast beef. Here's how:

Chop up the fat trimmings, cover with water in a covered heavy pot, and cook over medium heat. When the fat begins to melt, remove the cover and cook over low heat until most of the fat has melted out and any bubbling stops. Strain the cooked mixture through a sieve into a bowl. Let cool. Skim off the solidified pure fat.

To make suet cakes, pour melted fat into muffin tins or small aluminum pie pans. Chill in the refrigerator until the fat hardens.

To serve, put the suet cakes in an old mesh onion bag. Tie the bag shut at the top and hang it from a tree branch.

# Table Feeders

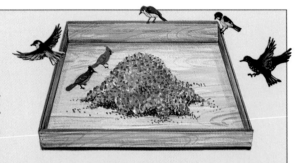

Many birds are picnickers. They like to eat on the ground. These birds like a tray or table-type birdfeeder. A table feeder can be as simple as a flat piece of plywood on bricks, a handy backyard stump, or a pair of split logs arranged flat side up.

Or you can build a simple table of your own.

A good size for a table feeder top is about 2 feet by 3 feet, with legs 6 to 12 inches high. A 3-inch-deep rim around the table top is sometimes helpful to keep the feed from washing away in rain or wind; and it's a good idea to have drainage holes at the corners to keep the feeder from filling up with water.

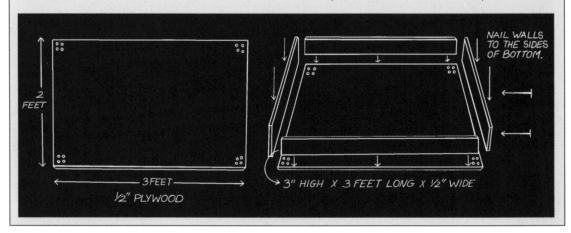

2 FEET

3 FEET

½" PLYWOOD

3" HIGH X 3 FEET LONG X ½" WIDE

NAIL WALLS TO THE SIDES OF BOTTOM.

◀ Feeders You Can
Make at Home

# THE ALL–PURPOSE BEAK

It's often possible to tell how or what a bird eats by the shape of its beak. Bird beaks, collectively, are a sort of biological Swiss army knife. Look at enough beaks and bills, and you'll see every conceivable kind of tool, from sledgehammers to spoons, harpoons, and needle-nosed tweezers. The pelican has a natural fish net — a big naked pouch that stretches from the front of its bill to its neck. With it, the pelican catches fish about once out of every three tries — which is better than most human fisherpersons. The crossbill uses its beak, which looks like a stepped-on pair of scissors, to snip seeds out of evergreen cones. The wading avocet uses its skinny turned-up bill like a scythe, swinging it back and forth in the water to uncover tiny creatures on the muddy bottom. Skimmers, who eat by whipping over the surface of the water, skimming a meal off the top as they go, look like they're in a permanent pout. Their lower (skimming) bills are much longer than their upper (clamping-down-on-the-catch) bills. Try sticking

## Southpaw Parrots

Unlike other birds, parrots use their feet like hands, to grasp food and carry it up to their mouths. And, like people, parrots prefer one "hand" over the other. Some parrots are right-handed; some are left-handed.

▲ Toucan

your lower lip way out and you'll get the idea. Parrots and their relatives are living nutcrackers; and their hooked upper beaks do double duty as fruit slicers.

Generally, seedeaters, such as finches have short, solid, cone-shaped beaks, tough enough to crack open crunchy seed coats. Insect-eaters tend to have longer, thinner beaks, suitable for picking (scurrying) meals out of cracks and crevices in bark and leaves. Meat-eaters, such as hawks and eagles, have powerful hooked beaks that operate like combination scrapers and steak knives; and fish-eaters often have long, spearlike bills for grabbing or stabbing scaly swimmers. The crow probably has the bird world's best all-purpose beak. Crows are omnivores, which means that they eat practically everything, from mice to watermelons, plus bugs, lizards, eggs, potato chips, French fries, and corn-on-the-cob. Crow beaks are both long and sharp, and heavy and thick, set to grab a mouthful of anything going. (You're an omnivore, too, which is why you have all-purpose teeth: sharp incisors and canines for cutting and tearing; flat molars for grinding and mashing. If you were a bird, chances are you'd have a beak like a crow's.)

Though all bird beaks function mostly as hunting weapons, heavy-construction tools, and kitchen utensils, they're not as tough and unfeeling as they look. Beaks are alive. Beaks, part of the bird's skull, are made of bone. The beak bones are covered with horny keratin, the same protein that makes up fingernails, hair, and feathers. Beaks, though, are also full of touch-sensitive receptors and blood vessels, which means that they're much more

## The Roman Crow

The ancient Romans were really much better soldiers than sailors. When they did go to sea, they tried to fight their battles much as they did on land. Roman battleships carried a gangplank or boarding bridge, made with a curved hook at one end. With this hook, the Romans would latch onto an enemy ship; soldiers would then run across the boarding bridge to attack. Usually, since the Romans were such well-trained fighters, they won.

The Roman boarding bridge was called a *corvus*, the Latin word for *crow*, because the hooked end was shaped like a crow's beak.

## A Beak Hall of Fame

Flamingo

Crossbill

Golden Eagle

Skimmer

Wood Duck

Cockatoo

Finch

Avocet

Raven

like lips than fingernails. Robins use their sensitive beaks to *feel* in the ground for worms.

## The Upside Down Filter Feeding Flamingo

One of the strangest of all bird beaks belongs to the flamingo. Flamingos feed with their heads upside down in shallow water — and their beaks therefore operate upside down. Most birds' jaws operate pretty much like yours. Your upper jaw is fixed to your skull. When you eat, it's your lower jaw that drops open, allowing you to

## Winter Food

Squirrels aren't the only ones to store food for the winter. Woodpeckers, jays, Clark's nutcrackers, and nuthatches all stash nuts and seeds to tide them over the lean winter months. Woodpeckers jam acorns into holes in trees; nutcrackers bury pine seeds — up to 30,000 per season, four or five seeds in each little hole. Some owls store winter prey, putting it aside to freeze just like you might put a package of hamburger in your freezer. When food gets scarce, they thaw their frozen mice by sitting on them, as if they were incubating eggs.

## Please Don't Eat the Butterflies!

Birds quickly learn to lay off monarch butterflies. One meal of those orange-and-black beauties is a sure way to get very sick. Monarch butterflies contain chemicals called **cardiac glycosides.** These chemicals are heart poisons. Monarchs pick them up from the milkweed plants they eat. (Monarch caterpillars, striped orange, black, and white, are poisonous, too.) After one awful-tasting experiment, butterfly-eating birds never go near the nasty monarchs again.

They also avoid viceroy butterflies, which, though nonpoisonous, look enough like monarchs to make the birds stay away.

### How Is a Flamingo Like a Whale?

Both flamingos and baleen whales, such as the gigantic blue whale, are filter feeders, straining their food out of the water through horny plates inside their beaks or mouths. The lesser flamingo has a filter system so efficient that it can even trap single cells.

bite and chew. Most birds operate in this same way: A smaller lower beak moves up and down against a larger, stationary upper beak. In the upside-down flamingo, however, it's the other way around. The upper jaw does the moving, and the lower jaw stays still. With this upside-down beak, flamingos — like blue whales — are filter feeders. Their beaks are lined with rows of horny plates that work like sieves, straining yummy little edible creatures out of the water.

# STICK OUT YOUR TONGUE

Baleen whales pick up their 4½ tons of tiny shrimplike krill a day by simply swimming through the ocean with their mouths wide open. Flamingos have to work a little harder for their dinners. They pump water through the sievelike plates of their bills by rapidly lapping (four times a second; you try it) with their fat, fleshy tongues. In ancient times, these big tongues meant trouble for the flamingo. Roasted flamingo tongues were a favorite dish at imperial Roman banquets.

Most bird tongues are smaller and skinnier than those of the flamingos, but that doesn't mean that all bird tongues are alike. Tongues, in fact, come in almost as many peculiar shapes and sizes as beaks. The strangest

tongue in the bird world probably belongs to the woodpecker. Woodpeckers peck to get at insects living in wood — usually in the bark of trees. Once they've hammered out a hole with their beaks, they use their long sticky tongues to pick up the insects inside. Most woodpeckers can stick their tongues out more than twice the length of their beaks, some as much as four times. Woodpecker tongues are sticky, like flypaper, from a special gluey substance in their saliva. Some are barbed on the tip, like tiny harpoons. Between glue and barb, woodpeckers usually get their bug. When not jabbing after insects, the woodpecker's long tongue pulls back inside its head like a retractable tape measure, wrapping up and around the bird's skull.

The woodpecker's retractable tongue, so long that it wraps back around the inside of the head when not in use, shoots out like a sticky dart to stab tasty insects.

## Bright Bills

The world's most gorgeous beaks belong to the toucans of South America: huge, curved bills patterned in orange, green, red, yellow, and blue. These are designed for fruit-picking. With them, toucans can latch onto fruits dangling high in the tangled jungle canopy. The big beaks are also good for crushing up the fruit, once picked.

While toucan beaks are colorful all year-round in the southern hemisphere, up north, the beak of the Atlantic puffin is almost as bright at least in the spring and summer. The Atlantic puffin, nicknamed the "Sea Parrot," develops a bright-colored sheath over its bill during the breeding season, in show-offy stripes of red and yellow. The sheath falls off in the autumn.

The Puffin

## ▼ Stick Out Your Tongue

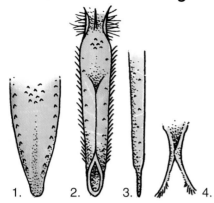

1. Shearwater
2. Red-breasted merganser
3. Wryneck
4. Bananaquit

## GULP!

The great blue heron eats not only frogs and fish, but also mice and gophers — which are always dunked in water before swallowing, to help them slide smoothly down the heron's gullet.

Sapsuckers, relatives of the sticky-tongued woodpeckers, drill holes in trees from which they sip sap, soaking it up through a hairy burrlike growth on their tongue tips. Hummingbirds also have long tongues, which roll up into little straw-like tubes, forming troughs for liquid nectar. Penguins have rough, spiky tongues. The spikes point backward, to keep slippery, swallowed fish from sliding back in the wrong direction.

Still, from a people point of view, all these clever tongues have one major drawback: Birds don't have many taste buds. Taste buds are the little clusters of sensitive cells on the surface of the tongue that make eating fun. Without them, all food would taste like sawdust. You have several thousand taste buds, capable of sensing four major types of taste: sweet, salty, sour, and bitter. The average backyard songbird, on the other hand, has just thirty to seventy taste buds; and Allen's hummingbird has only *one*. Birds, chances are, don't get to enjoy their dinners as much as you do.

# DOWN THE HATCH!

Birds not only don't taste as well as you; they can't swallow as well as you can, either. Did you ever see a heron swallow a fish? Birds lack a soft palate — that soft tissue on the roof of your mouth back toward your throat that

## SMASH!

Sea gulls like to eat clams and oysters, which they crack open by dropping them from great heights onto rocks. A pair of American pilots, downed off the northern coast of Canada, survived for ten months by eating seabirds' eggs and shellfish dropped and cracked by gulls.

Not everybody has been that lucky. The ancient Greek poet, Aeschylus, was killed by an eagle, who dropped a tortoise on his bald head, thinking that it was a likely tortoise-cracking rock.

helps you swallow. Unlike you, birds have to throw their heads back to swallow. They need help from gravity to get food from the mouth down into the esophagus, the tube that heads down toward the stomach.

# THE EYES HAVE IT

Before a bird can swallow a meal, of course, it has to find or catch it — and for that, most birds depend on their sharp eyesight. A bird, says one ornithologist, is really a pair of flying eyes. Birds see much better than people do. In fact, birds' eyes often weigh more than their brains. An eagle sees ten times better than you do: To be truly eagle-eyed, you'd have to be able to pick out a rabbit sneaking through the bushes two miles away. An owl at night sees 100 times better than you do. At times when you'd be stumbling around in the dark bumping into trees, owls are picking mice off the forest floor.

The reason for birds' super vision lies in the structure of the eye. You see because light passes through your pupil and falls on special cells on the retina at the back of your eyeball. These special cells turn the light into electrical impulses, which shoot up the optic nerve to your brain, and the brain tells you what you're seeing. You've got two main kinds of cells in your retina, named for their shapes: *rods* let you see in dim light; *cones* let you see in bright light and give you your color vision. You actually do pretty well vision-wise: You've got 125 million rods and 6 million cones in each retina of each eye, and you can see all the colors of

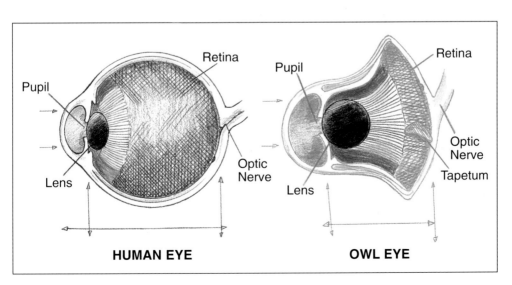

HUMAN EYE — Pupil, Lens, Retina, Optic Nerve

OWL EYE — Pupil, Lens, Retina, Optic Nerve, Tapetum

Birds have enormous eyes. Your eyes make up less than one percent of the weight of your head. A starling's eyes make up fifteen percent of its head weight.

Owls have the biggest eyes of all birds, relative to the size of their heads. If you were an owl, your eyes would weigh several pounds.

the rainbow. Not bad. Still, the night-hunting owl has ten times more rods than you do, plus a special membrane called a *tapetum,* that helps reflect extra light into the retina. It's the tapetum that makes owls' eyes glow in the dark. (Did you ever see a cat's eyes glow green at night when a light shines on them? That's their tapetum. Cats have one, too, which helps them see in the dark.) Daytime birds have more cones than rods. Sparrows, who need a sharp eye for zeroing in on seeds, have twice as many cones as you do.

Owls are unusual birds in that, like you, they have *binocular vision.* Binocular vision means that your eyes are set close enough together so that both see the same thing at the same time (overlap). This two-eyed vision is what gives you depth and distance perception. Most birds don't have this. Their eyes are set very far apart, which means they have a wider field of vision than people do, but little depth or distance judgment. Birds make up for this by cocking their heads: It's a way of eyeing something from different angles until they figure out how far away it is.

The woodcock, a chunky little brown game bird, literally has eyes in the back of its head. Its eyes are positioned so far around the sides of its head that it has a 360° field of vision — that is, without moving its head, it can see all the way around, front, sides, and back, plus up over its head. Woodcocks need to stay watchful; they've been hunted for centuries. The friendly cocker spaniel gets its name from its original job: hunting woodcocks.

## Birds' Field of Vision ▶ Compared to Ours

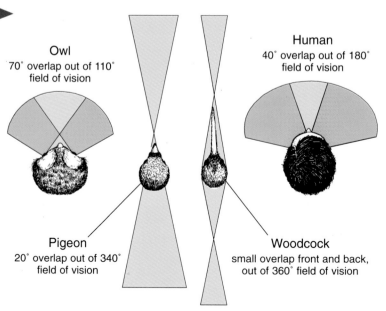

**Owl**
70° overlap out of 110° field of vision

**Human**
40° overlap out of 180° field of vision

**Pigeon**
20° overlap out of 340° field of vision

**Woodcock**
small overlap front and back, out of 360° field of vision

Bird eyes are well protected. For starters, birds have both upper *and* lower eyelids. In many birds, it's the lower eyelid that is most moveable. Hawks, for example, blink from the bottom up, while owls, like people, blink with the upper eyelid, from the top down. Birds also have a special transparent third eyelid, called a *nictitating membrane,* that moves sideways over the eyeball from the inside corner. When in place, the nictitating membrane is like a pair of goggles, protecting the eyes from wind while flying and from water while diving.

Nictitating Membrane

# INVISIBLE EARS

Some birds, especially owls, track down their prey by sound. Birds don't have outer ears. The *pinna*, the sound-collecting outside part of your ear, the part you hang earrings on or cover with earmuffs, is always missing in birds. (Birds need sleek, streamlined heads. Pairs of flapping ears would make too much wind resistance while flying.) Instead, birds just have openings covered with feathers on either side of their heads. The openings lead into long tubes that head back toward the eardrums. Owls, who listen for their food, have the biggest eardrums of all birds. These eardrums are particularly sensitive to sounds at frequencies of about 6,000 cycles per second. Scientists have found that that's the pitch of a mouse squeak. Owls also have uneven ears: One is set

## A Birdie Judges Depth

*A birdie with a yellow bill*
*Hopped upon my windowsill,*
*Cocked his shining eye and said,*
*"Ain't you 'shamed, you sleepyhead?"*
  —Robert Louis Stevenson (1885)

Birdies don't cock their shining eyes to talk to late sleepers. They cock their heads to make up for their lack of depth perception. Head-cocking allows the bird to view an object from several different angles, thereby figuring out how far away it is.

## Boom and Squeak

You can hear as well as or better than most birds. People can hear sounds ranging from about 100 cycles per second (the pitch of low booming noises like a bass drum) up to 20,000 cycles per second (the pitch of high shrill whistles). That's about what birds hear, too. Owls can hear sounds ranging from 100–18,000 cycles per second; starlings from 100–15,000 cycles per second. Mallard ducks hear in the range of 300–8,000 cycles per second — which means that ducks are missing out at the high end of the sound scale, and probably wouldn't appreciate piccolo music.

Many animals can hear a lot better than that. Bats can hear sounds at frequencies up to 30,000 cycles per second. Some moths can hear sounds up to 240,000 cycles per second.

higher than the other on the sides of the owl's head. This helps the owl figure out exactly which direction a squeak is coming from.

# WHAT DOES AN EARTHWORM SMELL LIKE?

Nobody is quite sure how well birds can smell. The champion smeller among birds is the New Zealand kiwi, whose nostrils are located at the very tip of its long bill. With them, the kiwi sniffs out earthworms. In other birds, the nostrils are located up close to the base of the beak, near the head. Most birds don't have much of anything in the way of noses — just a pair of holes in the beak. Shearwaters, petrels, and albatrosses, though, have tubenoses, which look like a pair of tubes on top of their bills, ending in nostrils.

Ocean birds use their noses for something even more important than smell. Ocean birds like albatrosses, murres, and gulls drink seawater, which is very salty. In most birds and animals, this would lead to problems. You, for example, can't live on ocean water; your body can't get rid of all the salt fast enough. All the seawater salt would build up in your blood and eventually it would kill you. (Remember that if you're ever lost at sea. Don't drink seawater. Drink rain.) Seabirds have special salt glands in their

▼ A Tubenose

nostrils, through which they quickly eliminate all that salt. Gulls are ten times better at getting rid of salt than you are.

# DIGESTING DINNER

Once a bird has found or caught its dinner, it has to digest it — which is quick work for a bird. A bird can digest a meal about seven times faster than you can, though not in quite the same way. When a bird first gulps down its food, the food goes into the *crop,* which is really just a storage compartment or holding zone. The crop is especially important for birds who eat on the run. It allows them to gobble down a big meal fast, before a predator pounces on them. The food is digested later, once the bird is safely home and out of danger. (Birds are like bank robbers making a quick getaway. First they stuff the loot in a sack and run. They sit down to count it only when they've made it back to their hideout.)

Once the bird is ready to settle down and digest, it's got two stomachs to do this with: the *proventriculus* and the *gizzard.* The proventriculus is a lot like your own stomach; it's where most chemical digestion of food takes place. The *gizzard,* on the other hand, is a must only for animals who don't chew their food. In birds, it substitutes for teeth. The gizzard is a mass of rubbery muscles lined with horny ridges that works as a powerful grinding machine, crunching up such tough tidbits as

## Phew!

The American turkey vulture, which eats carrion (that's a polite word for dead, rotting animals) finds its food by smell. In fact, the turkey vulture's sense of smell is often a big help to human engineers. Turkey vultures will gather around places where underground fuel pipes have cracked or broken — the leaking fuel smells like vulture food — and the clustered birds show repair people where the lines need fixing.

## The Curious Case of the Hoatzin

The crop isn't used for digesting food — except in the case of the peculiar hoatzin, a South American bird who lives along the edges of tropical streams. Hoatzins are about the size of pheasants, with blue faces, red eyes, and strange spiky crests that make them look like punk rockers. They are the only birds in the world who live on leaves — and leaves are hard to digest. Hoatzins only manage with the help of bacteria. In the hoatzin, the crop is fifty times bigger than the stomach and is full of bacteria, which break down the leaves into a form that can be absorbed by the hungry body. (This is the same way cows digest grass: gut bacteria do all the hard work for them.)

Since so much of the hoatzin's insides are taken up by this huge leaf-digesting crop, hoatzins are top-heavy. They can't fly very well, but they are good climbers and swimmers.

Their chief enemies are piranhas.

## Honeyguides and Beeswax

The African honeyguide, a relative of the woodpecker, is a brave bird. It gets its meals by attacking bee nests, where it eats the bee larvae and the wax that makes up the honeycombs. (It gets the name "honeyguide" because African natives follow it on its bee-tracking expeditions to find nests full of honey.) Very few animals can digest wax, but honeyguides, who have special wax-dissolving gut bacteria, can. Honeyguides can live for long periods of time on beeswax alone.

### Slurp!

Pigeons are the only birds who can drink water like people do — sucking it up against gravity. When other birds drink, they have to scoop up a mouthful of water and then tilt their heads backward to swallow.

acorns, fruit pits, grain seeds, and beetles. Birds sometimes swallow grit or stones to help the grinding process along — ostriches even gulp down ping-pong-ball-sized pebbles. (There's some evidence that dinosaurs had gizzards: Paleontologists have found small piles of rounded grinding stones associated with fossilized skeletons.)

Grebes and other fish-eating birds beef up their digestive processes by eating feathers. In fish-eaters, the gizzard isn't quite quick or powerful enough to grind up all those sharp little fish bones. Swallowed feathers seem to pad the bones and slow them down on their trip through the digestive system long enough for the gizzard to do the job.

In some birds, especially meat-eating birds, the gizzard not only grinds the food, it processes the leftovers. Owls, who swallow their prey whole, get a lot of indigestible stuff — like bones, teeth, and fur — along with the edible part of the meal. (Think of eating a cupcake with the paper wrapper still on it.) In the gizzard, these inedible rejects are rolled into tidy little packets called

### Bird Milk?

During the breeding season, the lining of the crop in some birds produces a special milky substance that is used to feed the babies. Baby pigeons (squabs), flamingos, and penguins are all fed on this form of "milk," which is made in the crops of both mother and father birds.

*pellets,* which the bird then coughs up and spits out. Ornithologists call this "casting the pellet." Hawks and eagles, who butcher their prey (they eat only the good parts) don't make pellets, but many other birds do, including crows, gulls, swifts, and kingfishers.

Other dinner leftovers end up in a form politely (and scientifically) called "bird droppings" — which occasionally make people extremely cross, especially when dropped upon newly washed cars. They also, occasionally, make people very rich. The Peruvian word for seabird droppings is *guano,* which, piling up in seabird colonies along the Peruvian coast, is one of the world's richest fertilizers. The Peruvian cormorant, a prize guano-maker, has been called the most valuable bird in the world. One hundred cormorants produce about a ton of guano every year. Peruvians have been collecting and selling guano for nearly 200 years.

## Squirting Birds

The fulmar may be the world's rudest bird. The Fulmar is a gull-like ocean bird who, in its proventriculus, makes a smelly reddish brown oil, which it squirts by the cupful at enemies. Long ago people who lived on the islands off Scotland used fulmar oil for cooking and lamp fuel.

## SCARE THE BIRDS

While birds spend most of their waking hours looking for dinner, people sometimes spend most of theirs trying to prevent them from getting it. Farmers and gardeners have been battling birds for thousands of years. The ancient Egyptians put up wooden frames covered with white netting to keep the quail away from their wheat. The ancient Chinese scared the birds away from their crops with firecrackers. The ancient Greeks set up purple-painted statues of

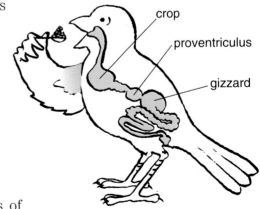

crop

proventriculus

gizzard

## PROJECT

# Build Your Own Scarecrow!

Here's what you'll need to build your own scarecrow:

- 1-inch by 3-inch board, about 5 or 6 feet long, sawed to a point at one end (scarecrow's body)
- 1-inch by 3-inch board, about 2 feet long (scarecrow's arms)
- Hammer and 1½-inch nails
- Old clothes
- Straw or rags for stuffing
- Rope or string
- Old white pillowcase

Center arms about a foot down from the top of the long board and nail the two boards together with three or four nails.

Put one leg of your scarecrow's pants over the bottom of the long piece of wood. Stuff both legs with straw or rags, and tie shut at the ankles and around waist. Put board arms through shirt sleeves. Button shirt and tie at waist with string. Stuff. Stuff white pillowcase to make the head. Add a face, using fabric crayons, markers, or paints. Slip open end of case over top of the long pole and tie with string.

Dig a hole about 1 foot deep, and sink pointed end of scarecrow into the ground; anchor it with dirt and stones.

Add a hat, bandanna, and garden gloves. For extra scare value, hang an aluminum pie plate from each arm.

## All that Glitters

Sometimes bird gizzards contain more than plain old pebbles. In 1911, hunters in Nebraska found gold nuggets in the gizzards of some ducks. Once the word got around, it set off a small gold rush. One story claims that the famous ruby mines of Burma were discovered after a ruby was found in the gizzard of a wild pheasant.

the god Priapus in their vineyards; the god was said to be so ugly that just one look at him would scare the birds silly. In case it didn't, the statues were armed with wooden clubs.

The medieval Italians scared the birds with animal skulls on poles; the Germans built wooden witches. Crops of the early American colonists were protected by small colonial boys, armed with rocks and pairs of boards, which they either threw or clacked loudly together. Nineteenth-century farmers preferred person-like straw-stuffed scarecrows, dressed up in cast-off clothes. These are what, in 1899, gave L. Frank Baum the idea for the friendly, but brainless, Scarecrow who went off with Dorothy and Toto to see the wonderful Wizard of Oz. Other anti-bird ideas have included whirligigs, flares, revolving spotlights, chemical repellents, recordings of bird distress calls, automatic exploders, delayed-action shotgun shells, and projectile bombs. Most recently, annoyed gardeners have tried to protect their plots with lifelike and life-sized plastic owls. Since owls eat smaller,

## The Unmentionable Bird

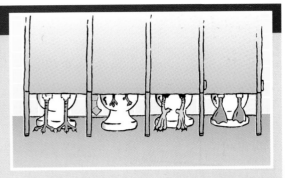

Birds don't pee like you do. You eliminate waste products from your body as either solid feces or liquid urine. The chemical that makes your urine yellow is **urea,** which contains poisonous ammonia, left over from the proteins in the food you eat. Birds don't make urea. Instead they get rid of ammonia by turning it into **uric acid.** Uric acid is not a liquid, but a solid. When you look at the bird splats on the windshield of your car, the dark-colored stuff is feces; the white stuff, crystals of uric acid.

Birds make solid uric acid instead of liquid urea because of their liquid-filled eggshells. Since fluids can't leave the eggshell, accumulating watery urea would surround and poison the baby bird before hatching. Uric acid, however, which doesn't dissolve in water, can build up inside the eggshell in solid form without hurting the developing bird.

seed-snatching birds, the sight of one perched threateningly on a fence post frightens thieves away. Unfortunately most birds are no fools and soon figure out that the motionless owl is a dud.

Birds' eating habits can work *for* people, too. Insect-chomping birds polish off enormous numbers of insect pests every year — and sometimes just in the nick of time. One famous saved-by-the-birds story is that of the Mormons and the California gulls. In 1848, the Mormons, led by Brigham Young, had just settled near the Great Salt Lake in Utah and had planted their first fields of crops. Before harvest time, to their horror, the fields were invaded by huge swarms of hungry crickets. It looked as though the crops were history — until flocks of cricket-eating California gulls swooped down and saved the day. Today the California gull is the state bird of Utah, and there's a statue in its honor in Salt Lake City.

Other birds helpfully pick off pesty rodents. Barn owls keep barns and farmyards free of grain-grabbing rats and mice. Owls in general, according to a British bird study, catch 23,980 rodents per year per square mile.

Which all seem like good reasons for us, in turn, to feed the birds.

# Eating Crow

People don't usually dispose of their crows by eating them, because crows, cooked, don't taste good. Nowadays if somebody says they're "eating crow," it means that they're humiliated and humbly admit that they are wrong.

The expression began, the story goes, back in the early nineteenth century with a real crow. During the War of 1812, an American hunter unknowingly crossed the British lines, and there, in enemy territory, he shot a crow. A British officer heard the shot, and tracked the American down with the intention of punishing him. Unfortunately, the officer wasn't really prepared to punish anybody, since he'd rushed out without his gun. He therefore complimented the hunter on his marksmanship and asked if he could have a closer look at his fine weapon. When the hunter foolishly handed it over, the officer pointed it at him, accused him of trespassing, and forced him, as punishment, to take a bite of his dead crow. He then gave the gun back, warning the hunter never to cross the British lines again. The angry hunter promptly trained his gun on the officer and made him eat the rest of the crow. The humiliated officer later reported the hunter to the American commander, demanding that he be punished for his action in crossing the lines. The commander called the hunter in to hear his side of the story and asked him if he had ever seen the British officer before. "Yes, sir," the embarrassed hunter replied. "I dined with him yesterday."

# Plant a Birdseed Garden

Grow your own birdseed! According to a U.S. Fish and Wildlife Service survey, the foods most widely liked by wild songbirds are black sunflower seed and white proso millet. Sunflower seeds are available from many seed companies. Plant the seeds about 1 foot apart, in 2-foot-wide rows, in an area that gets lots of sun. (Sunflowers may grow to be 12 feet tall; gardeners suggest that you plant them at the north end of the garden, where they won't shade other plants.)

For sources of sunflower seeds and other birdseed plants, see Appendix.

# BOOKS FOR BIRDFEEDERS

Baldwin, Edward A. ***Birdfeeders, Shelters, and Baths.*** (Storey Publishing; 1990)

*Plans for several simple birdfeeders, using such materials as tin cans and juice bottles.*

Crook, Beverly Courtney. ***Invite a Bird to Dinner: Simple Feeders You Can Make.*** (Lothrop, Lee & Shepard; 1978)

*Truly easy birdfeeders for beginners, including an egg carton feeder, a sugar sipper for humming-birds, and — from your leftover Christmas tree — a "Christmas tree hotel."*

Dawe, Neil. ***The Bird Book & Feeder.*** (Workman; 1988)

*Bird identification and feeding instruction book-let, with accompanying clear plastic feeder.*

Stokes, Donald and Lillian. ***The Bird Feeder Book.*** (Little, Brown; 1987)

*Instructions for attracting 23 different kinds of birds to your backyard feeder.*

Witty, Helen, and Dick. ***Feed the Birds.*** (Workman; 1991)

*Lists of bird food preferences and recipes for bird foods, with enclosed bird feed bag.*

# CHAPTER 5

# THE DAILY BIRD

◀ Tree-top Nesting

◀ High-Branch Nesting

A nest isn't really a bird home — it's a bird nursery. Nests are built for babies; you don't catch an adult bird nest-building unless he or she has offspring in mind. Baby bald eagles grow up in the world's biggest nests, which are immense shaggy treetop platforms, up to 10 feet across and 10 feet deep. Bald eagles re-use the same nest year after year, for batch after batch of eaglets, adding to it all the time until finally it becomes too heavy for the long-suffering tree and crashes to the ground. By that time, the nest may weigh as much as two tons.

Infant hummingbirds first see the light of day in the world's tiniest nests, fifty-cent-piece-sized little cups, woven of spider silk and thistledown. Young coots, jacanas, and grebes begin life in floating nests; young

## Yikes!

There was an Old Man with a beard,

Who said, "It is just as I feared! —

Two Owls and a Hen,

Four Larks and a Wren,

Have all built their nests in my beard!"

—Edward Lear
*Book of Nonsense* (1846)

**Low Branch, Bush, and Hollow Tree Nesting** ▶

**Ground Level Nesting** ▶

kingfishers hatch in a hole dug deep in the side of a riverbank. Some seabirds — terns, skimmers, murres, penguins — don't get much of anything in the way of a nest: They hatch on bare rock or in shallow holes scratched out in the sand. Uncomfortable as that sounds, they may be better off than baby owls. Owls are the world's worst nest-builders. Those that build nests put together muddled piles of sticks that sometimes fall apart, dumping eggs or owlets onto the ground. Luckily, not all owls build nests. Most small- and medium-sized owls nest in holes in hollow trees. The Western burrowing owl raises its family underground, in old badger holes or prairie dog tunnels; the tiny elf owl nests in holes in saguaro cacti; and the snowy owl of the treeless tundra nests right on the cold ground.

The most common kind of bird's nest is called a cup nest — named for its cup- or bowl-like shape. About three-quarters of common songbirds build this kind of nest. Cup nests are all put together in pretty much the same way, though depending on the habits of the bird builder, they may be located on the ground or on a window ledge, tucked in the shrubbery, or anchored in the branches of a tree.

## Crow's Nest

Crows are treetop nesters, building large platforms — really giant cups — of twigs and sticks high above the ground. A ship's lookout, positioned high up on the mast, must have reminded early sailors of the crows' nests in the trees back home. This lookout has been known as the *crow's nest* since the sixteenth century.

The Bettman Archive

Nests are made from the outside in. Usually the bird first builds a supporting platform, then works on the outer portions of the cup, shaping and tucking together bits of grasses, twigs, bark, and leaves. The inner cup is finished last, padded with mud, moss, hair, fur, feathers, and leaves, and, as a final touch, the mother bird molds it into perfect shape, settling down in the middle and slowly rotating around, tamping down the lining with her breast. (Leggy water birds, like herons, stamp their nests into shape with their feet.)

More ambitious birds, like kinglets and orioles, build hanging nests. These nests are dangling baskets, intricately stitched and woven together from plant fibers, grasses, and reeds. Often these baskets hang from the very ends of springy twigs and can be reached only by air, which makes them safe from most predators. Basket-weaving isn't simple. One Baltimore oriole spent forty hours building a nest, a job that involved some 10,000 stitches and the tying of thousand of knots, all with its

## PROJECT

### Dissect a Nest

In late summer or fall, well after the baby birds have taken off on their own, you may be able to find an empty bird's nest. Make sure the nest is abandoned; then, using tweezers, carefully pick the nest apart and analyze its components. What was used to line the nest? What was used to shape the outside? How many different materials can you identify?

## PROJECT

### Build Your Own Nest

A bird can do it — what about you?
Collect some nest-making materials
— grass, leaves, twigs, curls of bark,
thread, wool, bits of lichen and moss
— and try making your own cup nest.

beak. The African weaverbird works even harder, constructing a ball-shaped nest with a 2½-foot-long entrance tunnel, all woven from grasses.

## STICKS, STONES, AND RUBBER BOOTS

Birds are creative: They use all sorts of building supplies, both natural and man-made, in putting together their nests. Common materials include sticks, grasses, leaves, reeds, and bark, thistle and milkweed down, feathers, moss, lichens, wool, hair, and spider silk. Cliff swallows build neat gourd-shaped nests out of mud pellets, often fastened to a cliff wall, under the eaves of a house, or high on the underside of a bridge. Ovenbirds build two-roomed adobe globes that look a bit like old-fashioned Dutch ovens — which is where they get their name. Osprey nests are immense junk piles, accumulated year after year from sticks, seaweed, cow pats, and waterside rubbish: bottles, fish nets, old rubber

**Osprey Nest ▶**

O.S. Pettingill/Cornell Lab of Ornithology

## Using Up and Making Do

Chipping sparrows like to line their nests with horsehair. The tree sparrow uses ptarmigan feathers and lemming fur. Author John Steinbeck came upon an osprey nest in his garden which contained three shirts, a bath towel, and his very own garden rake; a pair of wrens, nesting in the rafters of a California office building, constructed their home of pilfered office sup-plies, including paper clips, rubber bands, and thumbtacks. This practice of using lit-tle stuff unwanted by others has a scien-tific name. It's called *autolycism* after Autolycus, a character in Shakespeare's play, *A Winter's Tale*. Autolycus was a great scrounger. Shakespeare called him a "snap-per-up of unconsidered trifles."

boots, straw hats, and tin cans. Hawks and starlings liven up their nests with green leaves, continually replaced as they wither and brown. Ornithologists believe these bird bouquets work as insect repellents, the leaves containing chemicals that fend off crawly pests.

Many birds do not build open nests, but prefer to live in cavities, either in holes made on their own or in holes ready-made by somebody else. (Some ornithologists think that birds only started building open nests because there just weren't enough holes to go around.) The best hole-makers among birds are the woodpeckers. And, since woodpeckers like to start each new year with a brand-new hole, there are always old holes available for other tenants. Woodpecker holes can be up to 2 feet in diameter and take anywhere from several days to several weeks to make. Nest-building great spotted woodpeckers will peck away for six hours a day; and black woodpeck-ers for even longer, males and females taking turns. Once

### PROJECT

## Nesting Time — Do Your Bit!

In early spring, help out the building birds by setting out a box of nesting materials. Include bits of string and yarn and small strips of cloth, cut 3–6 inches long. Many birds like hair — put out the combings from your hairbrush, or the fur left over from brushing your dog. Try pine needles, dried grass, or broom straws.

Set your materials out in a shallow box or basket.

String, yarn, and cloth strips may be hung from tree branches.

## Edible Nests

The cave swiftlet of Southeast Asia doesn't need to bother about collecting nest materials. It makes its own: Swiftlet nests are made entirely of saliva. During the breeding season, the swiftlet's salivary glands enlarge, secreting a sticky white substance that the bird uses to mold a cup-shaped nest. The nests are attached high up on the walls of caves, from where they are collected and sold to restaurants, which serve them up whole, floating in chicken broth, as "bird's-nest soup."

woodpeckers have used the hole for a season, raising their babies on a cozy bed of wood chips, they move out; and the abandoned hole is up for grabs. Many birds just wait for a chance to move in on an ex-woodpecker hole: Hole-snatchers include owls, nuthatches, chickadees, titmice, flycatchers, starlings, bluebirds, and wrens.

## PARASITES AND PIRATES

The hardest-working nest builder, next to the jack-hammering woodpecker, is probably the horned coot, a South American water bird who lives in lakes in the Andes Mountains. Before building a nest, the coot has to build itself an island — which it does by hauling stones, one at a time, from the mountains and dropping them in the water until an enormous rock pile is built up, reaching nearly to the surface. On top of this homemade underwater mountain, the coot builds a nest of water plants.

## Peter Peter Pumpkin-Eater

Like Peter of the old nursery rhyme, who shut his wife up in a pumpkin shell, the hornbills of Africa and Asia seal their mates up inside hollow trees. After mating, the female hornbill squeezes into the nest cavity, and the male plasters over the entryway with mud, leaving only a tiny hole, just big enough for the tip of the female's bill. Sealed in the tree, the female lays and hatches her eggs, fed by the male, who stuffs insects and fruit in through the breathing hole. About forty days later, once the babies are well along, the female breaks out by bashing down the mud wall. The babies promptly rebuild it and remain in the hole, being fed by their parents, until they are ready to fly.

On the opposite end of the scale, some birds get away without doing any work at all. These, including cuckoos, cowbirds, finches, honey guides, and even one species of duck, are brood parasites. They build no nests of their own, but instead sneak their eggs into other birds' nests, tricking the foster parents into raising their offspring. To do this, the European cuckoo works like a master spy, keeping a close watch on its intended victims as they build their nests and lay their eggs. She then waits for a moment when the nest is empty, quickly gets rid of the owner's egg (sometimes by eating it), and lays her own. The whole process only takes about ten seconds.

# PROJECT

## Build a Birdhouse

Bluebirds!

Hole-dwelling birds, like bluebirds, wrens, and chickadees, often like backyard nest boxes. A basic single-family nest box of the sort shown here is a favorite among many different species of birds. The plans outlined below, for a bluebird house, will also suit wrens, chickadees, titmice, and tree swallows.

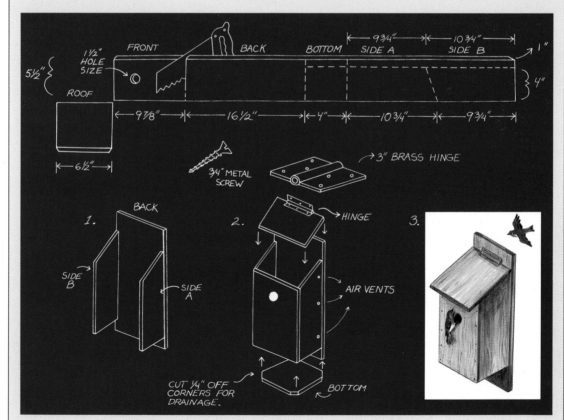

A cuckoo relative, the American Brown-headed Cowbird, lays up to five of her eggs in somebody else's nest. The young cowbirds hatch one or two days earlier than the nest-owner's babies, and, being bigger and stronger, often grab so much food away from them that they starve to death. Other birds raise their own babies, but steal a nest in which to do it. Some cowbirds, sparrows, and purple martins are nest pirates, throwing other birds out of their newly built nests and claiming the nests for themselves.

## BIRDS IN BUNCHES

Most birds are solitary, single-family nesters, but others prefer group living. Many seabirds, like petrels, gulls, murres, puffins, pelicans, and penguins, nest in huge colonies that may contain thousands of birds. Cliff swallows group their clay nests to make bird apartment buildings on cliffs or under bridges; great blue herons

## Grow a Birdhouse

Large gourds can make wonderful birdhouses. There's even one variety called the 'Birdhouse' (or 'Dipper') gourd because it has been so popular for this purpose. See Appendix for seed supplier.

Gourds are like pumpkins — they're vining plants that take up a *lot* of space. Plant seeds in groups of four or five, leaving 4 to 6 feet of space between seed groups. Harvest the gourds when completely ripe, wash thoroughly with a disinfectant, like Lysol, and spread out on newspaper in a dry, well-ventilated area. Don't let the gourds touch each other. Your gourds will take three to four weeks to dry. During the drying period, turn them regularly so that they will dry evenly.

Once the gourds are dry, cut a hole 1½ inches in diameter in the upper middle of

H.P. Smith, Jr./Vireo

the gourd for a doorway. Try to use gourds that are large enough so that there is at least 5½ inches of space from the bottom of the doorway hole to the bottom of the gourd. Otherwise your birds won't have enough space inside for nest building.

Attach a fastener to the top of the gourd and hang at least six feet above the ground from a porch roof, pole, or tree.

## Shared Nests

While some birds are nest pirates, stealing nests for themselves and kicking out the original owners, other birds manage to share. Some raptors let smaller birds like house sparrows build small nests on their larger nesting platforms. The sparrows then act as living burglar alarms, alerting their powerful neighbors at the approach of intruders. The raptors protect the sparrows from predators; and the sparrows themselves are safe because they're so close to home. Raptors usually don't hunt near their own nests.

cluster their stick nests together in trees. African weaverbirds like company — hundreds will hang their basket nests all from the same thorn tree. Some South American parrots build huge community nests, each weighing hundreds of pounds, divided into separate living compartments. In the eastern half of the United States, purple martins prefer to live together: Martin birdhouses contain many individual nesting rooms. Pigeons and doves are also group nesters. Pigeon-raisers house their birds in *dovecotes*, bird dormitories filled with many small rooms. It's from these little rooms that we get our word *pigeonhole*, meaning a little compartment in a desk, used for filing papers.

Purple Martin
Birdhouse

# THE MATING GAME

To a bird, a nest isn't much good without a mate — and a lot of (male) bird behavior is aimed at roping in a female. Male birds, each spring, go courting. Some birds try to win their mates with presents. A male snowy owl brings his chosen female a fat lemming — just like a young man might show up on his girl friend's doorstep with a box of chocolates. Terns bring fresh fish; jays bring acorns; bluebirds offer bugs.

Other birds try to win mates by showing off. Some display their fancy feathers: Peacocks and turkeys fan their tails; red-winged blackbirds flash their shoulder

# Blue Meteors

The biggest bird flocks ever seen were those of the passenger pigeons, the beautiful birds known to early American settlers as "blue meteors." Passenger pigeons were once the most abundant birds in the world. One early ornithologist estimated that one flock contained two billion birds. John James Audubon once watched a flock that took three days to fly overhead, at a rate of 300 million birds each hour.

All together, the passenger pigeons probably ate up to 43 billion bushels of nuts and seeds every day. In the breeding season, they nested in enormous colonies, some occupying over 200 square miles. So many hundreds of nests were built that the trees that held them sometimes collapsed under their weight.

During the eighteenth and nineteenth centuries, the passenger pigeons were slaughtered by hunters and their breeding areas destroyed with the clearing of the hardwood forests. The last known passenger pigeon, a female named Martha, died in 1914 in the Cincinnati Zoo.

The Cincinatti Zoo and Botanical Garden

# Birds of a Feather Flock Together

Birds flock because there's safety in numbers. Groups have a better chance of avoiding predators than a single bird on its own. Birds feeding in flocks always have a few lookouts ready to sound the alarm in case of danger. Even if a predator attacks, it often becomes confused by sheer numbers and can't manage to pick a single victim out of the enormous crowd. For this same reason — group safety — zebras run in herds and fish swim in schools.

# Pecking Order

Birds who live in groups are organized by rank, just like soldiers in the army. This organization is called **pecking order.** Pecking order was first discovered by a Norwegian psychologist named T. J. Schjelderup-Ebbe, who was studying chickens. In any group of chickens, he found that there was one VIP (Very Important Person) chicken who bossed all the rest, getting her own way by pecking. All the other chickens then fell into order, each being pecked by chickens ranking above her, and pecking at chickens ranking below her. The last chicken in line was out of luck, being pecked by everybody and able to peck nobody back.

All sorts of social groups of animals form "pecking orders," ranking themselves in order of power and importance.

patches; egrets raise their crests and plumes. Hawks, falcons, eagles, and hummingbirds put on spectacular aerial acrobatic acts. Many birds perform ritual "dances" before their future mates. The dances of the cranes are like elaborate ballets, though no human ballet dancer holds a candle to the crane, who can jump 20 feet straight up in the air. People have admired crane dances for centuries. Dancers in ancient China nearly 3,000 years ago performed the (crane-like) Dance of the White Crane.

Some wife-hunting birds do their courting in gangs. The males all gather at a traditional spot used year after year for courting parties. These hangouts are called *leks* (from an Old English word meaning play, as in playground), or *arenas*. There the males mill around waiting for females. When females appear, the males go into their act, hoping to attract the attention of a mate. In North America, the prairie chicken, the sharp-tailed grouse, and the sage grouse are all lekkers — as are the tropical jewel birds, birds-of-paradise, and the New Zealand kakapo, or owl parrot. Grouse mate-winning behavior involves dancing in circles, puffing out bright-colored balloon-like air sacs on their necks, and making booming mating calls. Lekkers seem to go in for short-term relationships: Birds who lek separate after mating, and the females nest and raise the babies all by themselves.

## Herds of Birds?

A crowd of cows is called a herd. Wolves run in packs; fish swim in schools; and bees fly in swarms. Did you know, though, that there are special names for different groups of birds?

- congress of crows
- covey of quail
- exaltation of larks
- gaggle of geese
- gulp of cormorants
- murmuration of starlings
- muster of peacocks
- nye of pheasants
- paddling of ducks
- parliament of owls
- sord of mallard
- stand of flamingos
- watch of nightingales
- wisp of snipe

## The Dance of the Rock Pigeon

Crane dances, with those 20-foot leaps, are too much for most people. Much easier is the dance of the rock pigeon. The male rock pigeon circles around the female in a series of little twirls or pirouettes, all the while nodding, bowing, and craning his neck.

## Halcyon Days

Today the word *halcyon* means quiet, calm, and peaceful — but to the ancient Greeks, the halcyon was a bird, the European kingfisher. The original halcyon, the Greek story goes, was a beautiful girl named Halcyone, daughter of the wind god Aeolus, who kept all the winds of the world locked up in a cave in the sea. Halcyone's husband was named Ceyx, and they were very much in love. One dreadful day, Ceyx was drowned at sea. Halcyone was so grief-stricken that she threw herself into the sea after him. The gods thought this so sad that they took pity on the lovers — and turned them into a pair of kingfishers. Zeus then ordered Aeolus to forbid the winds to blow for seven days before or after the winter solstice — the kingfisher's nesting season. These quiet, calm, and peaceful days are known as "halcyon days."

Other bird pairs are more faithful. Some — like swans, geese, eagles, ravens, Carolina chickadees, and common terns — mate for life. Most pairs only stick together through the spring breeding season, but some, like robins, may stay together for several seasons in a row. House martins and swallows are faithful to a nest site, rather than to a mate. Males return from migration first; if the female shows up at the nest site in time, the relationship may be on again. (If she's a slow flier, she may be out of luck.) Male ducks usually hang around only until the eggs are laid, then take off before the ducklings hatch.

# LOVE SONGS AND WAR CRIES

Spring, the breeding season, is a music festival of bird song. One springtime bobwhite sang 1,403 songs in a single day; a courting sparrow sang 2,305. And whippoorwills sing so often that, the story goes, turning somersaults in time to their singing will cure hiccups. No bird would spend so much time doing something just for fun. Bird song is serious business: It's communication. Birds sing to attract mates, to keep other birds away from their nests, to gather the flock together, to warn the neighbors of approaching danger.

## Most Talented Bird

The male bowerbirds of New Guinea and Australia probably go to the most trouble to attract a mate. There are eighteen species of bowerbirds, and each builds and decorates its own special bower, intended to catch and keep a passing female's eye. Bowers may take several months to make. Some are flat platforms, 8 feet across; others are woven arbors on bases of moss or 10-foot-tall "maypoles," trailing streamers. Some are approached by walled walkways or avenues. Once built, the bowerbird decorates his masterpiece with colored scraps: butterfly wings and beetle shells, bits of fruit and fungus, flower petals, and snail shells, plus trinkets pinched from people. Bowerbirds like buttons, keys, clothespins, socks, colored paper, and ballpoint pens. Most bowerbirds are especially fond of anything blue. The satin bowerbird — who has bright blue eyes — paints the walls of his bower blue, using bark dipped in a paint made from chewed blue berries, saliva, and charcoal.

Singing is not just the language of birds — it's also the bird version of the burglar alarm, the dinner bell, and the PA system.

According to ornithologists, there are two kinds of bird song: *songs* and *calls*. Calls are used for delivering information and are generally short and simple: Examples are warning calls ("Run! Owl!") and food-finding calls ("Get over here! Munchies!"). Many calls — like the chirping babble you hear when a flock is feeding — are placement calls ("I'm here. Where are you?"). Food-hunting pairs of parent birds call back and forth during their daily rounds just to keep in touch with each other, in the same way that people make telephone calls. Some backyard songbirds have languages of up to twenty different calls, each with its own special meaning. Crows (who, ornithologists say, are smarter than the average bird) use about sixty-four different calls and signals.

Songs are much more complicated than calls. Songs are the serenades of the bird world, used by musical males to woo their mates. About three-quarters of all songbirds not only sing, but have *repertoires* of two or more different songs. The song sparrow knows eight to ten songs; the brown thrasher over 3,000. Songs, ornithologists believe, *evolved* from competition among males for females: Over time, the better singers got the

## The Living Alarm Clock

Everybody knows about the rooster's wake-up call, delivered just before sunrise. The ancient Greek word for rooster was *hemerophonos*, which means day-sounding. The ancient Roman writer Pliny claimed that human beings owed all their achievements to roosters; without the rooster's crow, he said, people would never have gotten out of bed.

There are many calls in the language of roosters other than the famous early morning "cock-a-doodle-doo." "Gogogogok," for example, is a rooster alarm call, meaning danger is approaching on the ground ("Fox!"). "Raaay!" means danger from the air ("Hawk!").

better mates and the better nest sites, and therefore had more babies, while the not-so-good singers often got no mates at all. Eventually, over hundreds of thousands of years, elaborate bird-song melodies developed.

Bird calls are *innate* — that is, birds don't have to learn how to call; they know how by instinct. Songs, on the other hand, have to be learned. (It's the same in people. Babies are born knowing how to howl for food, but they have to learn how to sing "Twinkle, Twinkle, Little Star.") Most young birds learn how to sing from their fathers. The learning process can take weeks or months. Young birds at first jabber and babble — bird baby talk — and then become better and better, until they can sing as well as the grown-ups. Canaries need up to nine months' practice to learn to sing. Birds raised in isolation, never hearing an adult bird sing, never learn to sing properly themselves.

Human speech, even in the same language, varies from place to place. Depending on where you come from, you may speak English with a British or Spanish accent, with a New England twang, or with a Southern drawl. Bird songs also show these local differences, which ornithologists call *dialects.* Texas cardinals sound different from Minnesota cardinals. Rufous-sided towhees east of the Mississippi sing one kind of song; rufous-sided towhees from the Rockies sing another; and those from

## Polly Wann'a Cracker?

Like song birds, parrots have to learn to "talk," by listening and imitating what they hear. Parrots can't really talk, in the sense of carrying on a conversation. They're just very good at copying sounds. The world champion talking bird is an African Gray Parrot (named Prudle), who has a vocabulary of 1,000 words.

A person who *parrots* is somebody who simply repeats the words of somebody else without knowing what they mean.

New research at Purdue University, however, suggests that some parrots may be smarter than we think. Scientists there have taught Alex, a young African gray parrot, the names of 23 different objects (including water, paper and ink), five different colors, four different shapes, and the numbers 1–5. Alex can also accurately use a number of verbal commands, including "want", "come here", and "tickle me", and — when he wants the curious researchers to go away and leave him alone "no".

the West Coast another still. Sometimes the dialects become so different that birds of the same species can't understand each other anymore. In one experiment, a recording of an alarm call of Pennsylvania crows was played for French crows. The call made the French crows gather instead of running away.

Not all birds are as tuneful as songbirds. Crows squawk and croak — which is why, when you have a raspy sore throat, you're said to be *as hoarse as a crow.* Ducks quack; hens cackle; and gulls scream. Screech owls are named for their shrill shriek, though as screeches go, the champion screecher is probably the peacock. The peacock's call is a spine-chilling scream; the National Zoo in Washington, D.C., continually gets complaining calls about peacock racket. The saw-whet owl has a grating cry that sounds like a saw being sharpened. Geese honk; trumpeter swans trumpet; whooping cranes whoop; and loons laugh.

If you have a beautiful singing voice, chances are that people will tell you that you sing like a bird — but that's not true. You sing (or talk or holler) with your *larynx* or voice box, which is located up at the top of your windpipe. The larynx contains a pair of hard membranes (your vocal cords) that vibrate when air passes over them, creating sound. Put your fingers on your throat

## The Story of Syrinx

In Greek mythology, Syrinx was a nymph, a beautiful nature spirit. One day Pan, the great god of the forests, fell in love with her. Pan was a very ugly god. He had curly horns, pointed ears, and goat legs, covered with shaggy fur. Sometimes, when Pan was disturbed or in a bad mood, he would give a blood-curdling scream, so terrifying that all within hearing distance would run away mindlessly in fear. Our word *panic*, which means mindless terror, comes from Pan and his dreadful screams.

Syrinx didn't like Pan at all, and when he began to chase her, she ran away. To hide herself, she leaped into the river and turned herself into a reed among all the other reeds growing along the river bank. The reeds made a soft musical sound as the wind blew through them, and Pan was enchanted. He cut some of the hollow reeds and tied them together to make the first panpipe, or syrinx. As he played upon it, he told himself that he and his beloved nymph were singing together.

### The What's & Where's of the Windpipe & Syrinx

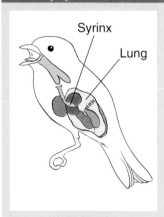

Syrinx
Lung

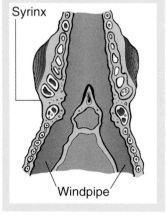

Syrinx

Windpipe

while talking, and you'll be able to feel your vocal cords vibrating.

Birds sing — or squawk or screech — with a *syrinx.* The syrinx is located at the bottom of the bird's windpipe, inside the bird's chest, and is made up of soft stretchy membranes. Songbirds have eight or nine different pairs of muscles that pull on these membranes, adjusting their tension like a drummer tightens or loosens the skin on his drum. At the same time, the bird can control the air puffing through the syrinx from the lungs, in ways that change the pitch, rhythm, and volume of the song. Birds can sing louder than you can. Birds can also sing with their mouths full; and they can sing two different notes at the same time. The two sides of the syrinx are controlled independently, each using air from a different lung. Birds can therefore sing simultaneous double tones, one note on the left side and another on the right. They can harmonize with themselves.

## TERRITORIAL TUNES

Bird songs aren't always love songs. Sometimes songs are fighting words. Birds sing to warn other birds off their home ground. This marking off of property is called *territoriality.* (You're a territorial animal, too. Did you ever hang a Keep Out sign on the door of your room or shoo a strange dog off your lawn?) Not all birds have the same idea about what territory means. Territory sizes vary

# Make Your Own Birdcall

Here's what you need to make your own birdcall:

A piece of bamboo, 1 inch in diameter

A piece of bamboo, ⅜ inch in diameter

A bottle cork

Sandpaper

A small piece of soft cloth

Fine string

Note: Bamboo is available from most craft stores.

**1.** Cut the 1-inch-thick bamboo between the nodes to get a single piece, 9-½ inches long.

**2.** Cut the narrower piece of bamboo to get one length 11 inches long, with a node at one end.

**3.** Carve a little slit 4 inches from one end of the wider piece of bamboo. Carefully enlarge the slit to form a round opening.

**4.** On the side opposite the carved V, starting ¾ inch from the end of the tube, carve an angled mouthpiece opening as shown.

**5.** Slice the cork in half lengthwise. Sand the rounded side of the cork so that a 1-inch length is beveled.

**6.** Shove the cork into the mouthpiece end of the wide bamboo. The flat side of the cork should be toward the round opening in the front; the beveled side toward the mouthpiece in the back. Poke the cork into the bamboo tube until about ¼ inch shows through the front V hole. Cut off any extra cork sticking out the top.

Sand the mouthpiece and the beveled end of the cork so that the edges are smooth and tight.

**7.** Carve a narrow groove all around the thinner bamboo, about ¾ inch from the end without the node. Put a pair of cotton balls on either side of the bamboo, just above the carved groove. Wrap the cotton balls in a small circle of cloth and tie tightly in place with your fine string or thread. The string should sit in the carved groove. This is the stopper for your birdcall.

**8.** Insert the stopper into the wide bamboo tube. As you blow in the mouthpiece, pull the stopper up and down. Try to tweet like a bird.

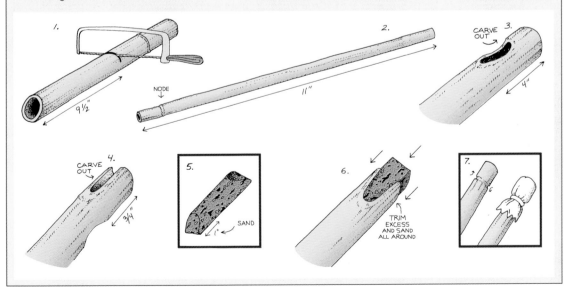

Sometimes bird territoriality works for people. Since the Middle Ages, geese have been kept as family watch birds, ready to rush out hissing and pecking at the sign of an intruder.

hugely from species to species. Golden eagles defend enormous territories of up to 35 square miles; least flycatchers defend about 700 square yards; gulls and penguins defend a few square feet around their nests. Hummingbirds defend favorite patches of flowers, chasing off other hummingbirds and invading butterflies.

Bright feather colors are also used as territorial "keep out" signs. The robin's red breast and the red-winged blackbird's red shoulder send a signal to other robins and blackbirds: NO VACANCY. If push comes to shove, birds will fight fiercely to defend their homes, shoving, lashing, pecking, and biting.

# IT'S A BIRD'S LIFE

Birds are usually thought of as early risers. If you *get up with the chickens* or *rise with the lark,* that means you're up and out at the crack of dawn. *Early birds* are the ones that catch worms; and at least twenty different species of songbirds greet the dawn with song. Depending on which bird you're talking about, though, *up with the birds* may mean not crawling out of the sack until suppertime. Many bird species are nocturnal: Many (not all) owls, nighthawks, and nightingales are night birds. If you're a *night owl,* you like to stay up late at night, and *to fly with the owls* has meant to roam around in the dark since the 1500s.

Whether day or night birds, most birds fill their waking hours in the same way. In certain months of the year, they keep themselves busy finding mates, building nests,

## Sing a Song of Sixpence

Sing a song of sixpence, a pocket
full of rye,
Four-and-twenty blackbirds baked
in a pie,
When the pie was opened, the birds
began to sing,
Wasn't that a dainty dish to set
before the king?

Live birds, during the Middle Ages, really were baked in pies. The pie was cooked with a filling of bran, to keep the crust from caving in. Then, just before bringing the pie to the table, the cook cut a hole in the bottom, drained out the bran, and, one by one, slipped in small live songbirds. When the pie was cut, the released birds would fly out and around the banquet hall.

More often, though, the birds were actually cooked. A pie containing twenty-four baked blackbirds probably served six, which was about average for a medieval pie.

## Swan Song

The white swans usually seen in park ponds are mute cousins of the North American trumpeter swan. A legend dating back to ancient Greece says that just before these silent swans die, they burst out into beautiful song. The Greeks thought this celebrated the bird's joyous departure to join Apollo, the god of music.

Today, any artist's last work is commonly called a swan song.

## Old Birds

### Recorded Life Spans

| | (Years) |
|---|---|
| Bald eagle | 21 |
| Blue jay | 18 |
| Canada goose | 23 |
| Herring gull | 27 |
| Northern cardinal | 15 |
| Red-tailed hawk | 19 |
| Red-winged blackbird | 15 |
| Ruby-throated hummingbird | 6 |
| Birder (male) | 70 |
| Birder (female) | 77 |

defending their territory, raising their young. Every day they spend hours foraging for food — if you were a bird, you'd spend most of your time grocery shopping. Birds preen daily to keep their feathers in prime working order. They squabble. They take baths.

And how long does all of this activity go on? Generally, small birds don't live as long as large birds. In the wild, most hummingbirds and small songbirds barely make it to their first birthday, though some may live to reach three or four. Caged birds live longer. Pet canaries, for example, may live 15 to 20 years. Slightly bigger birds, like robins and jays, have life spans of 10 to 20 years; gulls live about 30 years; doves, pigeons, and pelicans, 30 to 40. Hawks, eagles, and owls may make it into their fifties and sixties; crows, ravens, and swans may live to be seventy. The longest-living birds on record belong to the parrot family: cockatoos may live to be 80 or older. One African gray parrot made it to 93; an Amazonian parrot to 102!

## Most Popular Bird

The most popular cage bird in the United States is the Australian parakeet — sometimes called the budgerigar or budgie. Budgies are bright, friendly little birds who come in many colors: yellow, green, blue, violet, and gray. Parakeets are parrots and are also clever talkers, with vocabularies of up to 400 words.

In the 1950s, there was an American craze for parakeets: One out of every five American families had one of their own. At the height of the craze, parakeet owners could buy parakeet pants for their pets, along with parakeet sweaters trimmed with rhinestones, parakeet leg bands made of silver, parakeet tote bags (for outings), and even — for departed parakeets — tiny coffins.

Alan, Sandy. ***The Plaid Peacock.*** (Pantheon; 1965)

*The plaid peacock hatches just as some bagpipers march by, and eventually becomes their mascot.*

Atwater, Richard and Florence. ***Mr. Popper's Penguins.*** (Little, Brown; 1938)

*Mr. Popper, who has always wanted to be an explorer, receives a penguin as a present from an Antarctic expedition.*

Bang, Molly. ***The Paper Crane.*** (Morrow; 1987)

*A stranger pays a poor restaurant owner with a magical paper crane.*

Baylor, Byrd. ***Hawk, I'm Your Brother.*** (Scribner's; 1976)

*Rudy adopts a hawk in hopes that he too will learn to fly.*

Cowley, Joy. ***The Duck in the Gun.*** (Doubleday; 1969)

*A mother duck nests in a cannon and stops a war.*

Fatio, Louise, and Roger Duvoisin. ***Hector Penguin.*** (McGraw; 1973)

*Hector Penguin falls out of a truck on the way to the zoo and ends up in a forest, where none of the animals knows what a penguin is.*

Fleischman, Sid. ***The Scarebird.*** (Greenwillow; 1988)

*A special yellow-eyed scarecrow helps Lonesome John make a friend.*

Gerstein, Mordicai. ***Prince Sparrow.*** (Four Winds; 1984)

*A sparrow, who might have been a prince, turns a very nasty princess into a good queen.*

Holman, Felice. ***Elisabeth, the Birdwatcher.*** (Macmillan; 1963)

*Elisabeth builds a birdfeeder, battles a persistent squirrel, and learns a lot about the visiting birds.*

Krueger, Kermit. **The Golden Swans.**
(World Publishing; 1969)

*A folktale from Thailand, in which a hunter captures a beautiful golden swan with a mysterious secret.*

Lionni, Leo. **Tico and the Golden Wings.**
(Pantheon; 1964)

*Tico is given golden wings by the wishingbird, but then gives all his golden feathers away doing good deeds.*

Macaulay, David. **Why the Chicken Crossed the Road.**
(Houghton Mifflin; 1987)

*The hilarious and convoluted story of why the chicken really crossed the road.*

McCloskey, Robert. **Make Way for Ducklings.**
(Viking; 1941)

*With the help of the police department, a mother duck and her ducklings cross the busy streets of Boston.*

Paterson, Katherine. **The Tale of the Mandarin Ducks.**
(Lodestar; 1990)

*A Japanese fairy tale about a beautiful mandarin duck who is coveted by an evil nobleman.*

Polacco, Patricia. **Just Plain Fancy.** (Bantam; 1990)

*An Amish girl is horrified when one of her plain hen's eggs hatches out a fancy peacock.*

Uchida, Yoshiko. **The Rooster Who Understood Japanese.** (Scribner's; 1976)

*Mrs. Kitamura's rooster, Mr. Lincoln, causes the neighbors to complain about his early morning crowing, so Miyo helps find him a new home.*

Yolen, Jane. **Owl Moon.** (Philomel; 1987)

*A little girl and her father go into the woods one moonlit night in search of owls.*

# BOOKS FOR MIDDLE-SIZED KIDS

Coerr, Eleanor. ***Sadako and the Thousand Paper Cranes.*** (Putnam; 1977)

*A little girl who developed leukemia after the bombing of Hiroshima tries to fold 1,000 paper cranes, since, according to Japanese legend, once the cranes are completed, the gods will make her well again.*

Colum, Padraic. ***The White Sparrow.*** (McGraw-Hill; 1972)

*A pure white sparrow hatches out in Paris, learns all the ins and outs of bird life, and ends up building a nest in the elephant statue at the Trocadéro Museum.*

George, Jean Craighead. ***The Cry of the Crow.*** (Harper & Row; 1980)

*Mandy adopts and tames a wild crow, and then experiences the pain of freeing and losing her bird.*

George, Jean Craighead. ***Gull Number 737.*** (Thomas Y. Crowell; 1964)

*Luke and his ornithologist father watch the bird of Gull Number 737 in the laboratory, and Luke later uses his knowledge of gulls to help solve the problem of bird-caused plane crashes.*

George, John and Jean. ***Dipper of Copper Creek.*** (E. P. Dutton; 1956)

*While spending the summer in the Colorado Rockies prospecting for gold with his grandfather, Doug becomes fascinated with the water ouzel, or dipper bird. He later saves a dipper fledgling that has been caught in a rock slide.*

Keith, Harold. ***The Blue Jay Boarders.***
(Thomas Y. Crowell; 1972)

*Tom, Joey, and Susan take over the care of a nest of orphaned baby blue jays — with the surprising help of Beaky, the town bully.*

Lawson, Robert. ***I Discover Columbus.***
(Little, Brown; 1941)

*An irreverent account of Columbus's voyage of discovery, narrated by a New World parrot, Aurelio.*

Leichman, Seymour. ***Freddie the Pigeon: A Tale of the Secret Service.*** (Doubleday; 1972)

*Freddie the Pigeon solves a mystery, dealing with such peculiar characters as the sinister Dr. Sydney, Felicia, an angel in sneakers, and Litness the Catlike Birdman.*

Mowat, Farley. ***Owls in the Family***.
(Little, Brown; 1961)

*The story of Wol and Weeps, two adopted owls who turned a Canadian family (and town) topsy-turvy.*

Ormondroyd, Edward. ***David and the Phoenix.***
(Follett; 1957)

*David meets the Phoenix while mountain climbing and, riding on its back, has wonderful adventures with witches, sea monsters, griffins, and fauns.*

Pinkwater, Manus D. ***The Hoboken Chicken Emergency.*** (Simon & Schuster; 1977)

*Arthur brings home Henrietta, a giant chicken, for Thanksgiving dinner, and the family keeps her as a pet instead.*

Rolerson, Darrell A. ***A Boy Called Plum.***
(Dodd, Mead; 1974)

*Rudyard, who lives on a small island in Maine, raises a blue heron named Kite.*

Stanger, Margaret A. ***That Quail, Robert.***
(J.B. Lippincott; 1966)

*The (true) story of an adopted quail who answers the telephone, eats at the dining room table, sleeps in the Christmas tree, and generally takes over his (her!) human family.*

Stolz, Mary. ***Pigeon Flight.*** (Harper & Row; 1962)

*Mr. Pigeon (Monitor of the Head of William Tecumseh Sherman) is kicked off his statue in the park, so he and his wife set off to explore the country.*

# Talkative Birds

Aiken, Joan. ***Arabel's Raven.***
(Doubleday; 1974)

*Arabel's pet raven, Mortimer (who says
"Nevermore!"), sleeps in the refrigerator, eats on
the stairs, hunts for diamonds in the coal scuttle,
and generally disrupts the Jones family.*

*Further adventures of Arabel and Mortimer can be
found in the sequels Arabel and Mortimer (in
which Mortimer nabs King Arthur's sword from an
archaeological dig) and Mortimer's Cross.*

Andersen, Hans Christian. ***The Nightingale.***
(Scholastic; 1986)

*The classic story of the Emperor of China and his
singing nightingales, real and artificial.*

King-Smith, Dick. ***Harry's Mad.*** (Dell; 1984)

*Harry inherits a very special and very talkative
parrot named Madison from an uncle in America.*

White, E.B. ***The Trumpet of the Swan.***
(Harper Collins; 1970)

*Louis the trumpeter swan is born without a voice,
but learns to play the trumpet so that he can win
the beautiful Serena.*

# NAME THAT BIRD!

I'll give you a hint, I'm not very popular with the mice.

Mike Hopiak/Cornell Lab of Ornithology

◄ **Can you name the mystery bird?**
*See page 113 for answer.*

As you begin your bird-watching career, chances are that you'll first learn to know the birds by their common everyday names. Some of these names (see pages 112 and 113) are based on the birds' calls or colors; others on the way the birds behave. Woodpeckers, for example, peck holes in trees. Flycatchers nab insects on the wing. (One species — the brown-crested flycatcher — also nabs an occasional hummingbird.) The osprey gets its name from the Latin *osifraga,* or bone breaker; this name, one bird authority explains, was co-opted from the lammergeier, an Old World vulture that drops bones onto rocks from great heights, shattering them so that it can eat the inner marrow.

Sparrow comes from an old Anglo-Saxon word meaning *flutterer,* which is what sparrows spend a lot of time doing. Mockingbirds are copycats, mocking the calls and songs of other bird species. Hawk comes from the same Old English root as the word *have,* meaning to grasp or grab, which is what hawks do to their prey. Goatsuckers (relatives of

▲ "Lewis and Clark's First Glimpse of the Rockies"

whippoorwills and nightjars) are unfairly named for something they never did; a false rumor dates back to the ancient Greeks who claimed that these birds sucked milk from the udders of goats. They don't; most have big bristle-edged beaks that they use like butterfly nets to scoop insects out of the air.

Some common bird names are derived from a distinctive bird body feature. (If you've ever been called Four-Eyes, Red, Shorty, or Moose, you'll sympathize.) Spoonbills are named for their broad spoon-shaped bills, which they swish through the water, feeling for food. The name *falcon* comes from the Latin *falx,* which means sickle; it refers to the falcon's bladelike beak and talons. The stork is named for its sticklike posture; the word *stork* comes from the same Anglo-Saxon root as the word *starch,* both meaning stiff as a board. Grosbeaks have big beaks; longspurs have an extra-long spurlike claw on their hind toes.

Then there are the seventy-seven different North American birds who are named for people. Often these names come from the explorer or naturalist who first formally identified the bird in the wild. Clark's nutcracker and Lewis's woodpecker were first described by William Clark and Meriwether Lewis on their famous cross-country trip to the Pacific Ocean in 1804–1806. (They didn't bring any live nutcrackers or woodpeckers home with them, but they did send President Jefferson four live magpies, one sharp-tailed grouse, and a prairie dog.) Steller's jay — a feisty dark-crested western relative of the eastern blue jay — is named for the German naturalist George Steller, who went along with Vitus Bering on the voyage that discovered the Bering Strait between Alaska and Russia in 1728.

Wilson's plover, storm petrel, phalarope, and warbler are all named for the famous ornithologist Alexander Wilson — a Scottish schoolteacher who came to America in 1794 and immediately fell in love with American birds (though the first thing he did after getting off the boat was shoot a woodpecker). The "Baird" of Baird's sandpiper was Spencer Fullerton Baird, scientific head of the Smithsonian Institution in the 1880s and a birder since the age of 16. The "Franklin" of Franklin's gull was Sir

## The Man Who Painted Birds

John James Audubon is America's most famous painter of birds. The son of a French sea captain, Audubon was born on April 26, 1785, on the Caribbean island of Haiti. When he was little, John James spoke French and was known as Jean Jacques. His father hoped that John James would become a sea captain, too, but the water made young Audubon seasick. All John James really wanted to do, from the time he was a boy, was to draw and study birds and other animals.

Young Audubon came to America in 1803 to manage the family estates in Pennsylvania, but he spent most of his time drawing pictures of North American birds. Soon he was travelling all over the country, searching out new birds. On one of his trips he met Daniel Boone, who taught him how to hunt squirrels. Audubon himself soon became so good at life in the wilderness that he was nicknamed "The American Woodsman."

Over the years, Audubon not only painted portraits of birds, he kept journals full of detailed notes on bird biology and bird behav-ior. He watched snowy owls fishing and wood ducks courting; he tracked flocks of wild turkeys and counted nesting swallows. (Once he found 9,000 in a hollow sycamore tree.) He travelled to Florida, where he drew ibises and flamingos; he went to Labrador, where he drew gulls and gannets (and was bitten by an angry puffin). In 1826, Audubon's collected drawings were published, in his best-known book, *The Birds of North America*. All the birds in it were shown life-sized; so the original book was enormous. (It measured 39 inches wide and 26 inches long, a size referred to by printers as "double elephant.") His journal notes were published separately, in a five-volume series called *Ornithological Biography, or An Account of the Habits of the Birds of the United States*.

Audubon was the first naturalist to paint birds as they actually appear in nature, living their daily lives.

He died on January 27, 1851.

In 1992, a copy of Audubon's *Birds of North America* sold at an auction in New York City for $4,070,000.

---

John Franklin, polar explorer, who mysteriously disappeared sometime in the 1840s while searching for the Northwest Passage. Thomas Brewer of Brewer's blackbird and Edward Harris of Harris's hawk were both friends of John James Audubon (of Audubon's oriole, Audubon's shearwater, and Audubon's warbler).

# THE FORMAL BIRD

Along with their everyday names, each bird also possesses a formal *scientific name*. Awful as they look, complicated scientific names exist for a good reason. People have been naming animals and plants for centuries, giving them the simple ordinary names that scientists call

## Plain Birds, Fancy Names

### How many of these birds can you name?

Bald eagle (Haliaeetus leucocephalus)

Black-capped chickadee (Parus atricapillus)

Blue jay (Cyanocitta cristata)

Canada goose (Branta canadensis)

Common barn owl (Tyto alba)

Crow (Corvus brachyrhynchos)

Herring gull (Larus argentatus)

Red-headed woodpecker (Melanerpes erythrocephalus)

Red-winged blackbird (Agelaius phoeniceus)

Robin (Turdus migratorius)

Harold Wilson

1.

Lang Elliot

2.

P.Stettenheim

3.

4.

Mary Tremaine

All Photographs on pages 112-113 Cornell Lab of Ornithology

5.

Art Biale

6.

Allen Cruickshank

7.

O.S. Pettingill

8.

Bill Dyer

9.

J. Robert Woodward

THE MYSTERY! BIRD

10.

Mike Hopiak

| | |
|---|---|
| 10. Common barn owl | 5. Robin |
| 9. Red-winged blackbird | 4. Blue jay |
| 8. Red-headed woodpecker | 3. Black-capped chickadee |
| 7. Herring gull | 2. Canada goose |
| 6. Crow | 1. Bald eagle |

## Birds with Nicknames

Some birds get their names from human nicknames. Robin is a short form of Robin Redbreast. Redbreast refers to the bird's rust-colored tummy, while Robin is an old nickname for Robert, as in Robin Hood, whose real name was Robert of Lockesley.

The mag in magpie is a nickname for Margaret; the jay in blue jay is a form of a common Roman name, Gaius. Purple martins get their name from the English proper name Martin; petrel is a short form of Peter. Guillemot, an Atlantic seabird, is a short form of the French Guillaume, or William. Guillemot means Billy.

common names. *Robin, blue jay,* and *woodpecker* are all common names — and so are *sunflower, snapdragon, potato,* and *elephant.* The problem with common names is that they're different from place to place — or, even more confusingly, the common names may stay the same from place to place, but they may refer to different things. In England, for example, a robin is a small thrush, about 6 inches long, with a rusty red breast. The American robin — named by early settlers because it looked like the robins back home — is also a thrush, but it is a much bigger bird: about 10 inches long, with a red breast and a black-and-white throat. The Australian robin, on the other hand, is not a thrush at all, but a flycatcher, though it still has a robin-like rusty red (or sometimes yellow) breast.

The confusing name problem was solved by a Swedish botanist named Carl Linnaeus who, in the eighteenth century, invented a successful system for classifying (and naming) all living things. Scientists had been trying to do this for centuries, but none of their systems so far had worked very well. Some scientists classified plants and animals by size: big, medium-sized, or small. Others tried dividing plants and animals into groups based on whether they were domesticated (cows, chickens, corn) or wild (lions). Linnaeus came up with a system in which plants and animals were methodically categorized in standard ways, according to their biological characteristics. His system is still used today.

In Linnaeus's system of classification, all living things are first divided into large general groups called *Kingdoms.*

You, your dog, and the robins in your back-yard are all members of the Animal Kingdom; tomatoes, daisies, and oak trees are all members of the Plant Kingdom. Kingdoms are then divided into *Phyla*, which in turn are divided into *Classes*. This dividing and sorting goes on and on, the groups getting smaller and smaller, and more and more specific. Finally each living thing ends up with two precise names, in Latin. This two-name technique is known as *binomial nomenclature*, from the Latin *bi* (two) and *nomen* (name). This two-part name assigns each living thing to a *genus* and a *species*. A genus is a whole group of living things of the same type; a species is one particular kind of living thing. Bears, for example, all have the genus name *Ursus*, since they are all related kinds of animals.

Tack a species name — *maritimus* — onto *Ursus*, however, and you've got a very particular kind of bear: *Ursus maritimus*, the polar bear.

The science of classifying plants and animals — fitting each one into its proper group — is called *taxonomy*. Ornithologists don't have it easy here, since, worldwide,

## Classify Yourself! Find Your Place in the Universe!

| | You | Robin |
|---|---|---|
| Kingdom | Animal | Animal |
| Phylum | Chordata | Chordata |
| Class | Mammalia | Aves |
| Order | Primates | Passeriformes |
| Family | Hominidae | Muscicapidae |
| Genus | Homo | Turdus |
| Species | sapiens | migratorius |
| Common name | Bob | Robin |

## The Little Botanist

Carl Linnaeus was born in 1707, in the town of South Rashult, Sweden, where his father was a clergyman and an avid gardener. Linnaeus was fascinated by flowers from an early age; by the time he was eight years old, he was known as "the little botanist." His scientific reputation as a botanist was made in 1732, at the age of twenty-five, after a plant-collecting trip to Lapland in northern Scandinavia, up beyond the Arctic Circle. It was an exciting journey: Linnaeus was shot at by hunters, accused of being a spy, and caught in a storm at sea; he also drank reindeer milk, ate moss, and was entertained by a musician playing a bagpipe made from a seal's stomach. When he got back home, one of the first things he did was have his portrait painted, proudly dressed in his explorer's gear, a fur coat, and curly-toed Lapp boots, and carrying a leather bag containing his inkstand, pen, microscope, and spyglass. He later wrote a book about the plants of Lapland, in which he began to develop his idea for a system for classifying all living things.

## Noisy Names

Many common bird names come from the sound of the bird's call, cry, or song. Bittern comes from an Old English word meaning *the bellowing of a bull*, and refers to the bittern's booming bray. Crane comes from the Anglo-Saxon *cran*, meaning *to cry out*; rail from an Old French word meaning *to make a scraping noise*. Whippoorwills, bobwhites, phoebes, peewees, crows, and curlews are all named in imitation of their calls; catbirds are named for their catlike meow; and warblers for their trilling song, full of tuneful quavers and runs. Hummingbirds are named for the hum of their rapidly beating wings; and the especially musical Calliope hummingbird is named for Calliope, the ancient Greek goddess of epic poetry. Its name means "beautiful-voiced."

## Sort the Birds

The birds (Class Aves) are generally divided into twenty-eight different Orders, based on their biological similarities and differences.

Tinamiformes...... Tinamous

Struthioniformes.. Ostriches

Rheiformes........ Rheas

Casuariiformes.... Cassowaries and emus

Apterygiformes.... Kiwis

Gaviiformes....... Loons and divers

Podicepedifores.... Grebes

Sphenisciformes... Penguins

Procellariiformes... Albatrosses and petrels

Pelecaniformes .... Pelicans and gannets

Ciconiiformes...... Herons, storks, ibises, spoonbills, and flamingos

Anseriformes ..... Ducks, geese, and swans

Falconiformes ..... Vultures, hawks, and eagles

Galliformes ....... Turkeys, chickens, pheasants, and quail

Gruiformes ....... Cranes and rails

Charadriiformes ... Gulls, auks, and waders

Columbiformes .... Pigeons

Cuculiformes ...... Cuckoos, roadrunners, and hoatzins

Psittaciformes .... Parrots

Musophagiformes.. Touracos

Strigiformes ...... Owls

Caprimulgiformes .. Goatsuckers and nightjars

Apodiformes ...... Swifts and hummingbirds

Coliiformes........ African mouse birds

Trogoniformes..... Trogons

Coraciiformes ..... Kingfishers, hornbills, and hoopoes

Piciformes ........ Woodpeckers and toucans

Passeriformes..... Perching birds, including the common backyard songbirds

# 1,000,000,000,000 Birds

Most of the world's birds are southerners: South America alone is home to 2,500 different species of birds and is sometimes called (by bird-lovers) the Bird Continent. Runner-up is Africa: about 1,750 species of birds live in the region south of the Sahara Desert. North America has 950 different species of birds. All together, scientists estimate, there are probably between 100 billion and 1 trillion birds in the world — that's 1,000,000,000,000 birds, enough to make a line stretching all the way from here to the sun and back again.

they have to sort out some 8,800 (or so) different species of birds. (On the other hand, *ichthyologists* — scientists who study fish — and *entomologists* — scientists who study insects — have it worse: There are 18,000 different species of fish and at least 2,000,000 different species of insects.) The Class Aves is divided into twenty-eight different bird Orders. The biggest of these orders is called *Passeriformes* — the perching birds — and its members include about half of those 8,800 bird species. (See box on page 116.)

## WHICH BIRD?

So how do you figure out which one of the world's trillion (or so) birds has landed on your birdfeeder? Most birders compare the bird at the feeder to the pictures and descriptions of birds in their handy *field guide* — an illustrated bird identification book, which includes descriptions of bird appearances, calls, behaviors, and geographical locations. A good field guide is an essential piece of equipment for serious birders.

## General Outlines of Some Birds ▶

Hummingbird

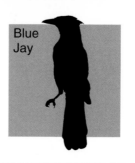

Blue Jay

Crow

## Avian Footwear

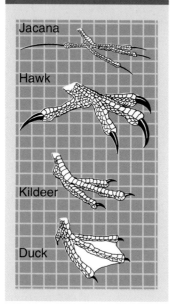

Jacana

Hawk

Kildeer

Duck

## Guide Books for Birders

Bull, John, and John Farrand, Jr.
**The Audubon Society Field Guide to North American Birds. Vol. I.** New York: Alfred A. Knopf, 1977.

Peterson, Roger Tory.
**A Field Guide to the Birds East of the Rockies.**
Boston: Houghton Mifflin Company, 1980.

Peterson, Roger Tory.
**A Field Guide to Western Birds.** Boston: Houghton Mifflin Company, 1961.

Scott, Shirley L., editor.
**A Field Guide to the Birds of North America.**
Washington, D.C.: National Geographic Society, 1983.

Udvardy, Miklos D. F.
**The Audubon Society Field Guide to North American Birds. Vol. II.** New York: Alfred A. Knopf, 1977.

## Map of a Bird ▶

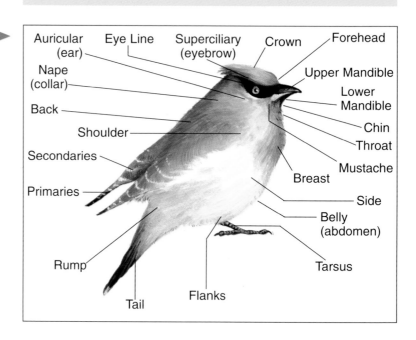

Auricular (ear) · Eye Line · Superciliary (eyebrow) · Crown · Forehead · Nape (collar) · Upper Mandible · Lower Mandible · Back · Chin · Shoulder · Throat · Secondaries · Mustache · Primaries · Breast · Side · Belly (abdomen) · Rump · Tarsus · Tail · Flanks

Duck

Ostrich

Owl

Eagle

## Here are a few pointers to help you name that bird:

1. Estimate how big your bird is. Is it small, medium, large, or simply enormous? Try comparing your bird to the sizes of birds you already know. Is it bigger or smaller than a robin? Is it about the same size as a sparrow or a crow?

2. What shape is your bird? Often you can figure out what family a bird belongs to just by its general outline. Check out the boxes above. See how many you know already.

3. Notice the shape of wings, tail, beak, feet. All of these are clues to a bird's identity.

4. Watch your bird's behavior. How does it fly? Does it flap, hover, or soar? Does it climb trees? Does it swim? Does it walk, waddle, or hop?

5. Finally, notice *field marks* — the stripes, streaks, speckles, and color patterns peculiar to your bird. Birds may have spotted bellies, white tail patches, stripes or circles above or around their eyes, patched or striped wings.

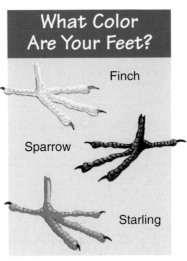
### What Color Are Your Feet?

Finch

Sparrow

Starling

## A Bevy of Beaks

Cardinal     Black-capped chickadee     Goldfinch     Hermit thrush     Hairy Woodpecker

## Colorful Names

Some birds are named for the color of their feathers. The hot pink flamingo gets its name from the Spanish word for flame. The orange or yellow oriole gets its name from the Latin aure-olus, which means golden. The cleverly camouflaged grouse is named from an Old French word meaning speckled or grizzled.

The gaudy, bright red (male) cardinal was named by sixteenth-century American settlers because its color brought to mind the bright red robes worn by the top officials — the cardinals — of the Roman Catholic Church.

## Pen Gwyn

The original penguin comes from the Welsh word pen gwyn, which means white head. Welsh sailors first gave this name to the great auk, a flightless relative of the puffin, once found throughout the North Atlantic, from Scotland to Newfoundland. The great auk was the first bird in the northern hemisphere since 1600 to become extinct: The auks were good to eat and were slaughtered by hungry sailors and whalers. Its name lives on, transferred to the (unrelated) penguins of the southern hemisphere.

The Bettman Archive

# PEERING AT THE BIRDS

To get a good look at the birds, most birders use *binoculars*. The first binoculars were invented in 1608 by a Dutch optician. They were big and heavy, and consisted of a pair of telescopes, clamped together side by side. Modern binoculars are much smaller and lighter. All contain prisms — wedge-shaped chunks of glass — which, by bending light rays, shorten the length of the optical tube needed and shrink the binoculars down to usable size.

Your binoculars should have some numbers printed on the eyepiece: say, "7x, 35" or "6x, 25." The first number (the 7x or 6x) tells you how powerful your binoculars are at magnification. At 7x magnification, for example, a bird will seem seven times closer to you than it really is. The second number (the 35 or the 25) gives you the size of the front lens of your binoculars: that is, the diameter of the lens in millimeters. The bigger this 2nd number, the bigger your lenses are and the more light that enters the binocular tubes, which means brighter, clearer images.

When it comes to binoculars, though, bigger isn't always better. Bigger lenses also mean that the binoculars are heavier and

### ▼ The Parts of Binoculars

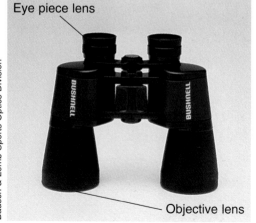

Eye piece lens

Objective lens

Bausch & Lomb Sports Optics Division

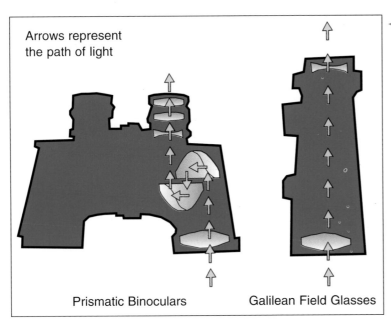

Arrows represent the path of light

Prismatic Binoculars          Galilean Field Glasses

harder to hold. The higher the magnification of your binoculars, the harder it is to hold them still, and at high magnification, a little wobble of your hands turns into a major wobble when you look at your bird. (*Really* powerful binoculars have to be mounted on a steady tripod.) Also, the higher the magnification of your binoculars, the smaller your *field of view*. The field of view is the area you can see through your binoculars. The bigger it is, the easier it is to get a bird into it. At high magnification, you need a much better aim, and it can be hard to zero in on a bird. You'll have to experiment to see which binoculars work best for you.

## BACKYARD BIRDS

In North America, the bird you're most likely to see through your binoculars is the red-winged blackbird. According to ornithologists, this is the most common bird on the continent, found all the way from the arctic tundra to Central America. You also probably have a good chance of seeing your state bird. Most states have chosen well-known common birds as their state bird — the sort of familiar bird that might hang out in your backyard.

Worldwide the most common bird is probably the European starling — which, thanks to Eugene Scheifflen and his fellow members of the American Acclimatization

# State Birds (or Count the Cardinals)

| | | | |
|---|---|---|---|
| Alabama | Yellowhammer (*Colaptes auratus*) | Illinois | Cardinal (*Cardinal cardinalis*) |
| Alaska | Willow ptarmigan (*Lagopus lagopus*) | Indiana | Cardinal (*Cardinal cardinalis*) |
| Arizona | Cactus wren (*Campylorhynchus brunnieicapillus*) | Iowa | American goldfinch (*Carduelis tristis*) |
| Arkansas | Mockingbird (*Mimum polyglottos*) | Kansas | Western meadowlark (*Sturnella neglecta*) |
| California | California quail (*Lophortyx californicus*) | Kentucky | Cardinal (*Cardinal cardinalis*) |
| Colorado | Lark bunting (*Calamospiza melanocorys*) | Louisiana | Brown pelican (*Palecanus occidentalis*) |
| Connecticut | American robin (*Turdus migratorius*) | Maine | Black-capped chickadee (*Parus atricapillus*) |
| Delaware | Blue hen chicken (*Gallus gallus var.*) | Maryland | Baltimore oriole (*Icterus galbula*) |
| Florida | Mockingbird (*Mimus polyglottos*) | Massachusetts | Black-capped chickadee (*Parus atricapillus*) |
| Georgia | Brown thrasher (*Toxostoma rufum*) | Michigan | American robin (*Turdus migratorius*) |
| Hawaii | Hawaiian goose (nene) (*Branta sandvicensis*) | Minnesota | Common loon (*Gavia immer*) |
| Idaho | Mountain bluebird (*Sialia currucoides*) | Mississippi | Mockingbird (*Mimus polyglottus*) |
| | | Missouri | Eastern bluebird (*Siala sialis*) |

Society (AAS), is now also an American starling, with a pesky population of around 200 million. Mr. Scheifflen and his friends were all Shakespeare fans, who, in the late 1800s, decided to bring to the United States every bird mentioned in Shakespeare's plays. One of the birds mentioned was the European starling. So, in 1890, the AAS released a crate of starlings in the middle of New York City's Central Park. The starlings loved the United States. By 1920, there were starlings all over the East Coast; by 1940, there were starlings on the Great Plains; and by 1950, there were starlings as far west and north as California and Alaska. By then, most American birders were mad at Mr. Scheifflen's starlings: All were big, noisy bullies who did a lot of harm to native American birds, mostly by stealing their nest holes.

Your chance of seeing a European starling is a whole lot better than your chance of seeing a bald eagle, our nation-

| | | | | |
|---|---|---|---|---|
| Montana | Western meadowlark (Sturnella neglecta) | Rhode Island | Rhode Island Red (Gallus gallus) |

Montana . . . . . . . Western meadowlark (Sturnella neglecta)

Nebraska . . . . . . . Western meadowlark (sturnella neglecta)

Nevada . . . . . . . . Mountain bluebird (Sialia currucoides)

New Hampshire . . Purple finch (Carpodacus purpureus)

New Jersey . . . . . American goldfinch (Carduelis tristis)

New Mexico . . . . . Roadrunner (Geococcyx californianus)

New York . . . . . . . Eastern bluebird (Siala sialis)

North Carolina . . Cardinal (Cardinal cardinalis)

North Dakota . . . Western meadowlark (Sturnella neglecta)

Ohio . . . . . . . . . . Cardinal (Cardinal cardinalis)

Oklahoma . . . . . . . Scissortailed flycatcher (Tyrannus forficatus)

Oregon . . . . . . . . Western meadowlark (Sturnella neglecta)

Pennsylvania . . . . Ruffed grouse (Bonesa umbellus)

Rhode Island . . . . Rhode Island Red (Gallus gallus)

South Carolina . . Carolina wren (Thryothorus ludovicianus)

South Dakota . . . Ring-necked pheasant (Phasianus colchicus)

Tennessee . . . . . . Mockingbird (Mimus polyglottus)

Texas . . . . . . . . . Mockingbird (Mimus polyglottus)

Utah . . . . . . . . . California gull (Larus californicus)

Vermont . . . . . . . . Hermit thrush (Catharus guttatus)

Virginia . . . . . . . . Cardinal (Cardinal cardinalis)

Washington . . . . . American goldfinch (Carduelis tristis)

West Virginia . . . . Cardinal (Cardinal cardinalis)

Wisconsin . . . . . . American robin (Turdus migratorius)

Wyoming . . . . . . . Western meadowlark (Sturnella neglecta)

al bird. Nowadays, the bald eagle is an endangered species in most of the United States. The bald eagle just squeaked in as our national bird, winning its election by just one single Congressional vote back in 1776. It appeared on the first American gold coins (the $10 gold pieces minted in 1795 were called *eagles)* and still appears, with olive branch, stars, and arrows, on the Great Seal of the United States, used on all official government documents since 1782. In second place after the eagle — the runner-up national bird — was the wild turkey, the bird favored by Benjamin Franklin. Wild turkeys, once common all over the eastern and southwestern United States, were threatened with extinction in the nineteenth century. Worried turkey-lovers banded together to bring back the turkey, and wild turkeys today are now going strong, found in wooded areas from New England west to the Rockies, and south to Central America.

Stock Montage, Inc.

## The Sterling Starling

The name starling comes from Old English and means "little star." The bird may have been given this name because the starling in flight, silhouetted against the sky, is star-shaped.

Sterling silver may get its name from the starling, after the four birds stamped on silver coins during the reign of Edward the Confessor, King of England from 1042-1066.

American Numismatic Society

## The Turkey Is Not Turkish

The turkey is not from Turkey any more than the American "Indians" come from India. It is, in fact, an all-American bird, and has been here since the Tertiary Period, some 60 million years ago. The first Europeans to lay eyes on the turkey were probably the Spaniards under Hernando Cortez, who landed in the Aztec area of Mexico in 1519. The Spaniards shipped turkeys back home, where, since nobody quite knew where all these explorers were landing, it was called the "Bird of India." The Germans and the Dutch, who got their turkeys from the Spanish and French, called them "Calcutta hens." The English, who didn't know where turkeys came from either, called them "Turkies" after the country of the same name. Turkey stuck, and so the name of our runner-up national bird today comes from a terrible mix-up in geography.

As a new birder, you should start — right now — your own *Life List,* which is a birder's personal record of all the species of birds he or she has ever seen, along with notes telling when and where the bird was spotted. An average Life List for a North American birder (especially one who has done a bit of travelling, binoculars in hand) usually contains somewhere around 400 different bird species. Really dedicated birders may see as many as 700 — which makes them eligible for the "700 Club," members of which all are expert bird-sighters. The present world champion of birders has done far better than that, though: the Life List of Harvey Gilston of Switzerland now contains 6,514 species — almost three-fourths of the world's known birds.

# DWINDLING BIRDS

Birders' Life Lists, scientists say, are likely in the future to get much shorter than they used to be. This isn't because birders aren't as quick on the draw anymore with their binoculars and guide books. It's because there aren't as many birds. Some biologists think that the number of eastern songbirds has fallen off in recent years by as much as 50 to 75 percent.

In 1962, Rachel Carson's frightening book *Silent*

# Draw the Birds

First, try to see your bird as a combination of simple shapes like circles, ovals, and triangles. Once you've sketched the basic shape of your bird, add more details, like eyes, beaks, and feet. Continue to add details — keep looking — until you have outlined all the parts of your bird. Finally add shading and color. Keep trying. Drawing, like so many other things, takes practice.

**Drawing a Puffin**

1.   2.   3.   4.

Drawing a male house sparrow standing, perching, and flying

BLACK
WHITE
GRAY
BROWN

GRAY CROWN
BROWN NECK
BLACK BIB

*Spring* showed how the use of pesticides, especially a chemical called DDT, was killing large numbers of birds. DDT and chemicals like it are particularly damaging because they are not easily *degraded,* or broken down — which means that DDT hangs around for a very long time. When birds eat DDT-contaminated food, the chemical settles in the tissues of their bodies. Unlike some pesticides, DDT doesn't usually kill birds off outright. Instead, it changes the way in which the birds' bodies process calcium, an element essential for making eggshells. DDT-poisoned birds lay eggs with very thin shells — so thin that

# DDT: Devil in Disguise

This is what DDT looks like to a chemist:

It's real name is Dichloro-Diphenyl-Trichloro-ethane (you can see why people call it DDT). Its anti-insect powers were discovered in 1939 by a Swiss scientist named Paul Muller. For this discovery, Dr. Muller won a Nobel prize.

In 1939, DDT looked like wonderful stuff. Farmers thought it would save their crops from crop-eating insects. Medical doctors thought it would save the world from lethal insect-carried diseases, like yellow fever, malaria, and typhus. At that time, the bad side of DDT wasn't known. Nobody knew it would kill the birds.

when the parent birds try to incubate their new eggs, the eggshells crush under their weight. All these crushed eggshells mean fewer and fewer baby birds — which in turn means fewer and fewer healthy adults. Particularly affected by DDT were brown pelicans, peregrine falcons, bald eagles, and golden eagles; and DDT was an important factor in the near extinction of the California condor.

Pesticides are still often poisonous to birds, but those in use today are much less long-lived than DDT. DDT has been illegal in the United States since 1972.

A more recent problem that birds face, however, is not that of environmental pollution. The present decline of the bird population, scientists believe, is due in large part to something that's happening far away: the destruction of the Central and South American rain forests. The rain forests are home to over half of the world's plants and animals — and nowadays, environmentalists estimate, they're being cut down at the rate of 100 acres per minute. That means that every minute we lose enough rain forest to cover fifty football fields. The cutting or burning of the rain forests not only destroys the homes of the tropical birds who live there year-round, it also wipes out the homes and feeding grounds of the North American migrant birds who spend their winters there. That's why many North American birds are disappearing: They don't survive their homeless winters. That's why bird-lovers all over the world are banding together to save the forests and save the birds.

# Save the Rainforests!

These groups are dedicated to helping save the world's rain forests:

## Rainforest Action Network

450 Sansome Street, Suite 700
San Francisco, CA 94111

This organization puts together letter-writing campaigns for rain forest preservation and supports the work of pro-forest groups in rain forest countries.

## The Rainforest Alliance

270 Lafayette Street, Room 512
New York, New York 10012

The Alliance provides information and educational resources about the world's rain forests.

## CAPE

PO Box 307
Austin, TX 78767

The CAPE Children's Rain Forest in Costa Rica is a managed forest project; Costa Rican kids help with the forest planting. For $5, you can plant a tree in the forest; collect $100, and you can protect a whole forest acre.

## Creating Our Future

398 North Ferndale
Mill Valley, CA 94941

Write this group for an information packet titled "How to Organize a Rain Forest Awareness Week at Your School."

# Save the Birds!

## Ducks Unlimited

One Waterfowl Way
Long Grove, IL 60047-9153

Ducks Unlimited is dedicated to the preservation of ducks and other waterfowl. For a $5 membership fee, kids not only help save the ducks, but receive a newsletter about waterfowl: the Puddler, for kids up to age 11, and Ducks Umlimited for kids 12 and older.

## Suncoast Seabird Sanctuary

18328 Gulf Boulevard
Indian Shores, FL 34635-2097

The Suncoast Seabird Sanctuary, dedicated to the rescue of sick or injured wild birds, is the largest wild bird hospital in the United States. You can help them out by adopting a bird of prey, brown pelican, sea gull, great blue heron, egret, cormorant or small land- or seabird, at a cost of $5–$10 per month. Write for further information.

## Wildcare, Inc.

RR 2, Box 338, Stonehouse Road
Rhinebeck, NY 12572

For $25, you can provide care for an injured owl for six months. Contributors receive a color photograph and life history of their adopted owl.

## International Crane Foundation

E-11376 Shady Lane Road
Baraboo, WI 53913-9778

The Crane Foundation sponsors an adoption program designed to protect endangered species of cranes. Write for information.

# FOR THE BIRDERS!

## BIRD LOVER'S SOCIETY

National Audubon Society
700 Broadway
New York, NY 10003-9501

## BIRD LOVER'S BOOKS

### Coloring Books

Bernhard, Annika. *State Birds and Flowers Coloring Book.*

Bonforte, Lisa. *Fifty Favorite Birds Coloring Book.*

De Leiris, Lucia. *Tropical Birds Coloring Book.*

Green, John. *Birds of Prey Coloring Book.*

*All are available from Dover Publications, Inc., 31 East 2nd Street, Mineola, NY 11501.*

### Activity Books

Stewart, Frances Todd, and Charles R. Stewart, III. *Birds and Their Environment.* Harper & Row Publishers, Inc., New York, 1988.
*This activity book contains fifty-three moveable bird stickers to be placed in the appropriate ecological setting: prairie, salt marsh, desert, bayou delta, Rocky Mountains. Comes with information booklet.*

*Gone Birding!* Available from The Nature Company, PO Box 188, Florence, KY 41022; 1-800-227-1114. *This bird identification game, with accompanying video, introduces players to 300 different birds. Can be played by all birders, amateur to expert.*

**The Hummingbird Game** (Ampersand Press, 691 26th St., Oakland, CA 94612; (800) 624-4263 or (415) 832-6669)

*A strategy game for young ornithologists. The game consists of sixty full-color illustrated cards: players attempt to match hummingbirds to food sources (flowers, insects) and habitat.*

**Wings on Strings** Mobiles. Order from Kaulfuss Designers, Inc., 325 West Huron, Chicago, IL 60610; (312) 943-2161.

*Three mobile kits are available: Songbirds 1, Songbirds 2, and Birds of Prey. Each easy-to-assemble mobile consists of six realistically colored and patterned folded cardboard birds. Kits come with information and activity sheets.*

# Bird Lover's Supplies

### Owl pellets are available from:

Insect Lore Products
PO Box 1535
Shafter, CA 93263
1-800-LIVE BUG

### A Birdseed Garden Seed Collection can be ordered from:

Seeds Blum
Idaho City Stage
Boise, ID 83706

### Birdhouse gourd seeds can be ordered from:

Stokes Seeds, Inc.
Box 548
Buffalo, NY 14240

Park Seed Co.
Cokesbury Road
Greenwood, SC 29647-0001

W. Atlee Burpee & Co.
Warminster, PA 18974

# Bird Song Tapes

Tapes of *Eastern/Central Bird Songs, Eastern/Central Birding by Ear, Western Birding by Ear* and *Know*

*Your Bird Sounds* including *Yard, Garden, and City Birds* are available from:

The Nature Press
40 West Spruce Street
Columbus, OH 43215

Tapes of *Bird Song and Bird Behavior, Florida Bird Songs, Common Bird Songs, Songs of Eastern Birds,* and *Songs of Western Birds,* each with a descriptive manual can be ordered from:

Dover Publications, Inc.
31 East 2nd Street
Mineola, NY 11501

# FOR AUDUBON ADMIRERS

## Biographies for Young Readers

Ayars, James Sterling. *John James Audubon: Bird Artist.* (Garrard; 1986)

Howard, Joan. *The Story of John J. Audubon.* (Grosset and Dunlap; 1954)

Kastner, Joseph. *John James Audubon.* (Walker & Company; 1994)

Roop, Connie and Roop, Peter. *Capturing Nature: The Writings and Art of John James Audubon.* (First Impressions; 1994)

Smaridge, Nora. *Audubon: The Man Who Painted Birds.* (World Publishing Co.; 1970)

## Postcards

*The Audubon Fine Art Postcard Book,* a collection of postcard-sized reproductions of many of Audubon's famous bird paintings, is available from:

KidsArt
PO Box 274
Mt. Shasta, CA 96067

## Activity Books

*Audubon's Birds of America Coloring Book* (48 pages) and *Audubon Bird Stickers in Full Color* (50 stickers in an 8-page booklet) are available from:

Dover Publications, Inc.
31 East 2nd Street
Mineola, NY 11501

# INDEX

Page references in *italics* indicate illustrations and photographs and those in bold indicate tables.